Second Edition

Getting Beyond "I Like the Book"

Creating Space for Critical Literacy in K-6 Classrooms

Vivian Vasquez

INTERNATIONAL
Reading Association
800 Barksdale Road, PO Box 8139
Newark, DE 19714-8139, USA
www.reading.org

The International Reading Association attempts, through its publications, to provide a forum for a wide spectrum of opinions on reading. This policy permits divergent viewpoints without implying the endorsement of the Association.

Executive Editor, Books   Corinne M. Mooney
Developmental Editor   Charlene M. Nichols
Developmental Editor   Tori Mello Bachman
Developmental Editor   Stacey L. Reid
Editorial Production Manager   Shannon T. Fortner
Design and Composition Manager   Anette Schuetz

Project Editors   Charlene M. Nichols and Christina M. Terranova

Cover   Design, Lise Holliker Dykes; Photographs (clockwise from top center), Vivian Vasquez and Shutterstock, © iStockphoto.com/Konstantin Tavrov, Shutterstock, © iStockphoto.com/Thomas Perkins

Library of Congress Cataloging-in-Publication Data

Vasquez, Vivian Maria.
  Getting beyond "I like the book" : creating space for critical literacy in K-6 classrooms / Vivian Vasquez. -- 2nd ed.
      p. cm.
  Includes bibliographical references and index.
  ISBN 978-0-87207-505-4
  1. Language arts (Elementary)--Social aspects--United States. 2. Literacy--Social aspects--United States. 3. Multicultural education--United States. 4. Critical pedagogy--United States. 5. Children--Books and reading--United States. I. Title.
  LB1576.V37 2009
  372.6--dc22

                                                                2009028546

SUSTAINABLE FORESTRY INITIATIVE
Certified Fiber Sourcing
www.sfiprogram.org

To the greatest love of my life, my little TJ,
who fills my days with more joy than I could ever imagine.
I dedicate this book to you.

CONTENTS

ABOUT THE AUTHOR

 **Vivian Vasquez** is an associate professor in the School of Education, Teaching, and Health at American University, Washington, DC, USA, where she teaches courses in critical literacy, children's literature, and early childhood education. Prior to this she was a public school and preschool teacher for 14 years. Although Vivian is no longer in the classroom, she continues to work with young children as a consultant and as a researcher alongside classroom teachers in the DC area. She received her doctorate from Indiana University, Bloomington, USA, her masters from Mount Saint Vincent University in Halifax, Nova Scotia, Canada, and her undergraduate degrees from the University of Toronto, Ontario, Canada, and from Lakehead University, Thunder Bay, Ontario. At the release of this book she will have worked as an educator for 25 years.

Vivian has held appointive and elected positions at the International Reading Association, the National Council of Teachers of English, the Whole Language Umbrella, and the American Educational Research Association (AERA). Other honors include winning the James N. Britton Award for her book *Negotiating Critical Literacies With Young Children*. This book also received the AERA Division B Outstanding Book Award.

Vivian was born in the Philippines, grew up in Canada, and currently lives in Maryland, USA, with her pride and joy, her five-year-old son, Taylor, and her husband, Andy.

Author Information for Correspondence
You can reach Vivian at vvasque@american.edu. You can also visit her website at www.vivianvasquez.com and view her podcast on critical literacy at www.clippodcast.com.

ACKNOWLEDGMENTS

I would like to thank my colleagues who contributed to this book: Susan Adamson, David Chiola-Nakai, Carol Felderman, Lee Heffernan, Kevan Miller, Michael Muise, Janice Shear, and Sarah Vander Zanden. Their insight and willingness to negotiate spaces for critical literacies in various contexts using different texts are an inspiration to us all. My deepest gratitude also goes to the children whose learning is described in this book and who have made our work as teachers both challenging and pleasurable.

This book was written with my invaluable colleagues and friends in mind, specifically Jerry Harste, Andy Manning, Barbara Comber, Allan Luke, Hilary Janks, Sonia Nieto, and Naomi Silverman. It has been such an honor to have kept your company. A special thank you also to those of you who unknowingly encouraged this revised edition through your support of the original text: Dorothy Menosky, Kathy Egawa, Brec Cooke, Stacie Tate, Liana Honda, Anna Sumida, and Kathleen Fay. Deborah Dillon, you recognized the potential for the first edition of this book and made it easy for me to grow it into the publication that it is today. Thank you for your sensitivity and support. You have a delicate touch that was much appreciated! Charlene Nichols, you were once again, as you were for the first edition, such an important part of this project. You took the stress out of the final moments in the publication process. Anne Fullerton, you encouraged this revised edition from the start. Thank you for your early encouragement and support. Finally, thank you to Shannon Fortner and Christina Terranova for making the final stages of production so enjoyable.

A special thank you to my family: Lily, Reggie, Vickie, Reggie Jr., Victor, Nanay, Uncle Jim, and Tita Chit for always being there for me. Andy Bilodeau, thank you for your "go for it" attitude, ongoing support, and technical help.

CHAPTER 1

Setting the Context: A Critical Take on Using Books in the Classroom

Patricia: Are you sure you looked?

Alexandro: Everywhere in there!

Patricia: She [the librarian] even helped me. She said, "I guess we don't have any."

Alexandro: Did you tell her that's not fair?

It was November. My kindergarten students and I had been together for three months and had gotten to know one another quite well. During this time I had attempted to construct a curriculum and make use of pedagogy to create opportunities for us to engage in a dialogue about diversity using the varied linguistic and cultural experiences and resources that this ethnically diverse group of children brought to the classroom.

The brief conversation between Patricia and Alexandro (the names of students that appear in this volume are pseudonyms) took place one day after returning from a visit to our school library. They had been looking for a book on the Philippines as one way to support Emma, a new student in the class, whose family had just moved to Canada from the Philippines. Their quest was met with frustration when they learned there were no books with characters who might be Filipino, nor were there any resource books on the Philippines. In a sense these children were learning about the notion of being "other," of not having spaces and opportunities to belong. Patricia's and Alexandro's frustration led me to suggest a class project focusing on the question, Do we see ourselves in books that are in our school library? A topic such as this may seem too difficult or complex for young children. For some children this may be true, however, from the beginning of the school year my students had available to them more powerful ways of talking about the world as I framed my teaching from a critical literacy perspective. This is also true for the other students and teachers you meet in this book.

Critical literacy has been a topic of debate for some time. Part of the debate is a response to attempts by some educators and researchers to pin down a specific definition for it. There is a belief among many critical literacy theorists and educators (Comber & Simpson, 2001; Comber & Thomson, 2001; Luke, 2007; Vasquez, 2001a, 2004) that as a framework for engaging in literacy work, it should look, feel, and sound different, and it should accomplish different sorts of life work depending on the context in which it is being used as a perspective for teaching and learning. In other publications, I have referred to this framing as a way of being, where I have argued that critical literacy should not be an add-on but a frame through which to participate in the world (Vasquez, 1994, 2000a, 2000b, 2000c). As such, there is no such thing as a critical literacy text. Rather, there are texts through which we may better be able to create spaces for critical literacies. Such texts are shared and discussed throughout this book. The world as text, however, can be read from a critical literacy perspective. What this means is that issues and topics of interest that capture students' interests as they participate in the world around them can and should be used as text to build a curriculum that has significance in their lives. Key tenets that comprise this perspective are as follows:

1. Critical literacy involves having a critical perspective (Vasquez, 1994, 2004).

   What this suggests is that critical literacy should not be taken on as a topic to be covered but rather should be a different way, lens, or framework, for teaching throughout the day. However, most teachers with whom I have talked about critical literacy have taken on this critical literacy perspective beginning with literacy instruction. As they become more comfortable teaching from this perspective they are better able to extend this way of being across the curriculum and throughout the day.

2. Students' cultural knowledge and multimedia literacy practices should be used (Comber, 2001; Vasquez, 1998, 2000c).

   Students learn best when what they are learning has importance in their lives. Using the topics, issues, and questions that they raise should, therefore, be an important part of creating classroom curriculum. Multimedia literacy refers to students' way(s) of making meaning in the world using combinations of print-based text and music, art, or technologically based text such as websites, videos, or podcasts.

3. The world is a socially constructed text that can be read (Frank, 2008).

   This tenet focuses on getting across to students the message that all texts are created by someone, somewhere, for some reason. The earlier that students are introduced to this idea, the sooner they are able to understand that texts can be revised, rewritten, or reconstructed to shift or reframe the message(s) conveyed.

4. Texts are never neutral (Luke & Freebody, 1999).

   What this means is that all texts are created from a particular perspective with the intention of conveying particular messages.

5. Texts work to position us in particular ways; therefore, we need to interrogate the perspective(s) of others (Meacham, 2003).

   Because texts are socially constructed and created from particular perspectives, they work to have us think about and believe certain things in specific ways. For instance, stories that portray females as being in need of rescue, such as Sleeping Beauty or Cinderella, work to convey messages that females are the weaker or less powerful gender.

6. We read from a particular position(s) and so our readings of texts are never neutral, and we need to interrogate the position(s) from which we read (speak, act, do...).

   Just as texts are never neutral, the ways we read text are also never neutral. When we read we bring with us our past experiences and understanding about how the world works.

7. What we claim to be true or real is always mediated through Discourse (Gee, 2005).

   Discourses are ways of being, doing, and acting through which we live our lives, and our understandings of the world—how we make meaning in the world—happen through these ways of being, doing, and acting.

8. Critical literacy involves understanding the sociopolitical systems in which we live and should consider the relationship between language and power (Janks, 1993).

   This suggests that part of our work in critical literacy needs to focus on social issues, such as race, class, or gender and the ways in which we use language to shape our understanding of these issues. How we use language to talk about such issues determines how people are able to—or are not able to—live their lives in more or less powerful ways as well as determine who is given more or less powerful roles in society.

9. Critical literacy practices can contribute to change and the development of political awareness (Freire & Macedo, 1987; Luke & Freebody, 1999).

   What this means is students who engage in critical literacies from a young age are likely going to be better able to contribute to a more equitable and socially just world by being better able to make informed decisions regarding issues of power and control.

10. Text design and production can provide opportunities for critique and transformation (Granville, 1993; Janks, 1993; Larson & Marsh, 2005; Vasquez, 2005).

    The explanation for this final tenet is deliberately more detailed as this is a tenet that is less talked about or written about, and yet this is the tenet that pushes us to move beyond critique and toward social action. Text design and production refer to the creation or construction of texts and the decisions that are part of that process. This includes the notion that it is not sufficient to simply create texts for the sake of practicing a skill. If students are to create texts they ought to be able to let those texts do the work that is intended. For instance, if students are writing surveys or creating petitions, they should be done with real-life intent for the purpose of dealing with a real issue. If students write petitions, they should be able to send them to the person for whom they were intended. Helping students understand real-life functions of text is an important component of growing as a critically literate individual (Luke & Freebody, 1999; Vasquez, 2005). Comber (2001) describes functional aspects of critical literacies as including the practice of using language in powerful ways to get things done in the world, to enhance everyday life in schools and communities, and to question practices of privilege and injustice. Critical literacy is also about imagining thoughtful ways of thinking about reconstructing and redesigning texts and images to convey different, more socially just and equitable messages that have real-life effects.

Do We See Ourselves in Books That Are in Our School Library?

The project that grew out of the conversation at the beginning of this chapter was an important one that raised questions of moral responsibility and established the role that our class could play in negotiating new, more equitable social spaces in our school and beyond.

Our school was pre-K to eighth grade with approximately 800 students. It was located in a middle-income neighborhood in a suburb of Toronto, Ontario, Canada. In our class of 18 students, we had 11 ethnicities represented, including children from Malta, the Philippines, and Peru. The children and I were therefore disturbed when we searched through the shelves of our school library over the next few weeks and discovered the following:

- There were no books on the Philippines.
- The books on Peru were outdated and were published in the 1970s.
- There were no books on Malta.

Earlier in the school year, I talked to the children about acting on issues that were of concern to us; that is, doing something about problems we face in the school community and beyond to contribute to building more democratic ways of being and doing in those places. At that time we made a list of possible types of actions, including finding out as much as we could about an issue to discuss and analyze it in a critical way. We talked about writing letters, doing research to find more information on a topic, and asking to meet with individuals involved to make our concerns public. We also looked at our own ways of doing and saying things and how we may have contributed to existing problems by not acting on them.

To address our concern regarding the lack of culturally diverse books in our school library, we engaged in a conversation regarding possible solutions. One suggestion made by a group of students was to write a letter to the librarian (see Figure 1). The letter makes public the findings of the students' discoveries in the library. Along with the letter, we attached a list of books with characters from diverse ethnicities and backgrounds and bilingual books that could be purchased for our school library. This list was created by one of the boys in the class together with his parents.

The librarian was very receptive to the letter. When presented with the findings, she appeared genuinely disturbed. Like many people, she had not thought about the marginalization of certain individuals and groups of students when they are unable to see themselves in books and other texts used in school. She immediately worked on ordering books to address our concerns. She also began rethinking the decisions she made regarding

Figure 1. Letter to the Librarian

Dear_____
Our class did
research
in the library
on books.
This is what
we found out.
The other paper
has books you
Should buy.

which books to display based on who is represented and not represented by those books.

As part of our project, we created a newsletter outlining the work that we had done. This newsletter was taken home by students and was one way of filtering our class inquiry into some of the children's homes. From the newsletter, Mena and her family began to explore how different cultures are represented by the way in which books are displayed at local bookstores. She and her parents talked to the manager of their neighborhood bookstore, emphasizing the need for books that represent diverse cultures to be available all year, not just for special events such as Black History Month or Women's History Month. Anthony and his mother questioned why children's literature was hidden in the back corner of their local bookstore and why a computer used to locate books was not available in the children's section as it was in other areas. It was amazing to learn about ways that my students had taken what they had learned in the classroom into their homes to engage in projects with their parents.

How This Book Was Originally Conceptualized and Then Expanded

Currently as an associate professor at the School of Education at American University I work closely with classroom teachers and preschool and elementary school children. Prior to this, I was a preschool and elementary school teacher for 14 years and as such I explored ways of framing curriculum from a critical literacy perspective. Common to both experiences are the connections I have kept with other classroom teachers. The motivation to connect was an interest in creating spaces for critical literacy. This book contains stories of my own experience in the classroom as well as the stories shared with me by classroom teachers who are colleagues and friends as we each embarked on a journey of exploring what critical literacy could afford our teaching and our students' learning. Like me, these teachers also wanted to know what difference it would make to frame our teaching from this perspective. They wanted to know what kinds of literate learners could be produced from this practice.

Consequently, the original version of this book, the first edition, was meant to make accessible to other educators our attempts (the teachers with whom I have worked along with my attempts) to create spaces for critical literacy in K–6 settings through the use of children's books. It is a collection of stories from classrooms where students and teachers have attempted to move their responses to text beyond the traditional "I like the book..." by putting a critical edge on their talk about books and other texts across the curriculum. The book consists of detailed critical literacy events and instances from classrooms as well as practical classroom strategies and lists of children's literature that can be used as sources to encourage and support critical conversations.

This second edition maintains the original classroom vignettes but updates some of the resources in connection with those stories as well as adds substance to the original text through the inclusion of three new chapters. One chapter focuses on science and critical literacy while another focuses on social studies and critical literacy. The third new chapter focuses on the intersection between new technologies, social media, and critical literacy. This is an element that makes this book unique. Over the years there have been growing accounts of critical literacy work in classrooms (Comber, 2001; Morgan, 1997; O'Brien, 2001; Vasquez, 1994, 1999, 2001b, 2005). Very limited in the literature, however, are accounts of the ways new technologies intersect with critical literacies. The chapter on technology included in this book is an attempt to bridge that gap.

Using Critical Literacies to Get Things Done in the World

In the opening vignette, we entered my kindergarten classroom where Patricia and Alexandro led the charge for changing the kinds of books that were made available in our school library. As they engaged in this act, they helped to break the pattern of privileging some students (those students who find themselves in books) while marginalizing others (those students, like Emma, whose experiences are not represented in the books available in the school library).

This project is reflective of Comber's (1992) findings that in classrooms where a critical literacy position is advocated, teachers respect student resistance and explore minority culture constructions of literacy and language and problematize classroom and public text. To respect student resistance and explore minority culture constructions of literacy and language, teachers provide space in the curriculum to address the diverse needs of students, including ensuring the curriculum speaks to the cultural ways of being of the students and the varied discourses (experiences with literacy, literate ways of being, and language use) that those students bring to the classroom. In our library project, for instance, we researched the lack of representation of particular groups of people in the books available at our school library. While problematizing classroom and public texts, teachers help students to interrupt and analyze texts that are often considered natural or neutral. For example, students and teachers together look closely at the illustrations and choice of words used in texts such as books and magazine advertisements. In our library project we disrupted the common practice of having on offer only those books representing the most dominant groups of people in our school as part of our school library book collections. The library project is an example of what happens when classroom work is framed from a socially critical approach to teaching and learning. Through this approach or perspective, students become or are positioned as researchers of language. In other publications I forefront the negotiation of critical literacies using everyday issues raised by my students (Vasquez, 2003a, 2003b, 2004, 2005). In this book I deliberately focus on critical literacy work that integrates the use of children's books. This decision was made for a number of reasons. First, print-based texts such as children's books are privileged in classrooms. Second, because books—whether these be picture books, chapter books, or basals—dominate the classroom, teachers are more used to working with those texts than they are working with other kinds of texts. Third, conversations with classroom teachers who have attempted to create space for critical literacy in their setting have predominantly used children's books to begin this process.

The stories I chose to include in this book focus on teachers' attempts at creating opportunities for critical literacies using literature in combination with other texts. Combining texts in this way moves us beyond traditional ways in which books have been used in classrooms and allows for more complex conversations. The title of this book reflects this sentiment. Specifically, the ways books are used on four particular fronts are presented. It is important to note that often while working from one front, other fronts are simultaneously addressed.

1. Pairing everyday texts with texts written for children.

   Everyday texts are real-world texts that can be found as part of daily living. These include newspaper clips, advertisement fliers, posters, greeting cards, and so on. In this book you learn about ways that these texts can be paired with texts written for children as one way to begin to negotiate critical literacy in the classroom.

2. Focusing on social issues by bringing the outside world into the classroom.

   Social issues are real-world issues that are important to children. In a couple of chapters you read about ways that classroom teachers have created spaces or opportunities for taking up these issues as part of the classroom curriculum.

3. Using children's literature to unpack social issues in the school community.

   Books are one of many tools that can be used to create space to discuss social issues that arise within the school or classroom. In several places in this book I share some of the ways that classroom teachers have used books along with other texts as a starting point for taking up and analyzing such issues.

4. Using children's literature critically in the content areas.

   Often, critical literacy has been discussed, written about, and promoted as something to be done as part of the literacy curriculum. Later in this book, I share instances of learning that demonstrate the role that critical literacy can play in the math, science, and social studies curricula.

5. Using technology as a communicative tool for sharing work done with texts.

   Larson and Marsh (2005) note that, "new information and communication technologies have changed, irrevocably, the nature and use of literacy" (p. 68). They further note that as a society we have taken a digital turn, and we need to take note of this in school settings. In this book, I have dedicated a chapter to focus on what it means to take on this digital turn and what this use of technology might look like in terms of doing literacy work in schools.

Children's Literature in Elementary School Settings

Children's literature has played a major role in elementary school classrooms for years. The widespread use of literature across the school curricula has created multiple opportunities for children and their teachers to interact with these literacy texts in a variety of ways, including critically reading books, as Patricia, Alexandro, and my other kindergarten students did when they raised concerns regarding the absence of particular kinds of books in our school library.

The take on critical literacy presented here is not about the books per se but what is done using books in different contexts and in combination with other texts such as posters and advertisements, as well as the kinds of perspectives brought to bear on talk about books. It is about creating opportunities for critical conversations and making available different social positionings for students as they engage with texts: "Social position considers how peers perceive each other as members of the learning community and as viable partners for specific literacy events" (Flint & Riordan-Karlsson, 2001, p. 5). *Texts* refer to books and everyday print and media publications such as magazine articles, advertisement fliers, and television commercials. Further explanation of everyday texts appears later in this chapter and in Chapter 2.

Working From a Theory of Language and Learning

The opening vignette offered a number of important insights into teaching and learning from a critical literacy perspective. When I asked Patricia and Alexandro why they felt it was important to have books on the Philippines or books that included characters that look Filipino, they offered two reasons. First, they said that having books on the Philippines was one way for them to learn about a country, and second, if there were no books with Filipino-looking characters, then it might be harder for Emma to tell her stories. When asked to clarify what "telling her stories" meant, they explained, "That means that Emma can say like in my home or like when this happened to me or that happened to me or that's not what I think and if there's no books with Philippines people then it'll be hard to say that." They continued by suggesting, "it isn't fair that other people are in books and Emma isn't." In other words, Patricia and Alexandro recognized that books present different kinds of realities: providing spaces for readers to connect their own experiences and understanding for purposes of reaffirming those experiences and understandings, or for taking issue with the realities that are presented for them. Further, they recognize that particular students' experiences and understandings are marginalized when they do not find themselves in books or when the realities presented do not represent their experiences.

Patricia and Alexandro are developing a critical perspective in the way that they use language to critique and in the way that they critique the language and images in books. How did they come to this perspective? In a sense, they have come to learn how to use language to critique in great part because of the critical discourses or analytical ways of being that have been made available to them in the classroom. For me, these ways of being are shaped in large part by the theoretical toolkit that informs my teaching and subsequently the Discourses (ways of being, doing, and talking) that my students learn.

Building a Theoretical Toolkit

I cut my critical literacy teeth in 1993 while taking a graduate course through Mount Saint Vincent University, which was being held during the summer at the University of South Australia. While in Australia my classmates and I had an opportunity to work with Barbara Comber and spend time with Jenny O'Brien. Barbara was finishing her doctorate with Allan Luke and exploring notions of critical literacy with him. She was also working with Jenny on creating opportunities for critical literacies in her classroom. At the time I had been framing my teaching from an inquiry-based perspective driven by whole-language principles (Watson, Burke, & Harste, 1989).

The more I talked with Barbara and thought about the kind of work Jenny was doing in her classroom, such as using Mother's Day ads as text, the more I imagined possibilities for critical literacy in my own classroom. Using their work in critical literacy as a lens through which to revisit some of my teaching practices led me to the realization that I was, on many instances, engaging in a naïve form of literacy teaching whereby I marginalized the social issues that my students were raising (Vasquez, 1994). In some instances, I downright ignored them. After that summer I was determined to listen to and observe differently what my students said and did and to attend more closely to the artifacts of their world that were interesting to them with an eye for opportunities to create spaces for critical literacy. For instance, while teaching kindergartners, one of my students questioned the use of toy packaging included in a fast food chain's kid's meal. Using the kid's meal as an artifact of learning, we deconstructed and analyzed the information on the packaging, asking questions like, Who would want this information? Why? What are the words and images on the package attempting to do to me as a consumer? (For more on this topic refer to Vasquez, 2005.) Barbara's work on negotiating critical literacies became part of my theoretical toolkit as I began to imagine possibilities for doing with my students social justice work in literacy. This imagining led me to read the work of Freire and other critical pedagogues (Edelsky, 2000; Freire, 1972; Freire & Macedo, 1987; Shor & Freire, 1987). Freire pushed me to think of what it means to "read the world" (Freire & Macedo, 1987, p. 29) and not just the word. He led me to be concerned about raising the "conscientizacao [critical consciousness] of learners" (Larson & Marsh, 2005, p. 41). However, Freire's work was primarily focused on adult learners and did not deal specifically with classroom practice, so I was thrilled when Luke and Freebody (1999) began their work on what came to be known as the Four Resources Model (refer to www.readingonline.org/research/lukefreebody.html for more information about the model).

In their model, Luke and Freebody (1999) assert that literacy is never neutral—that literacy is always situated within a series of ideologies or beliefs that shape what we do. While developing their model, they examined existing and proposed literacy curricula and pedagogical strategies. They state that effective literacy draws from a repertoire of practices that allow learners, as they engage in reading and writing activities, to participate in various "families of literate practices" (Luke & Freebody, 1999, p. 6). Freebody and Luke use the term *practices* to denote work that is actually done by literate beings in classrooms and beyond as an indication that these are negotiated, carried out, and achieved in everyday contexts unlike terms such as *schemata* or *competencies*, which denote a more individual, psychological model of literacy. In the Four Resources Model, four dynamic and fluid "families of (social) practices" (p. 6) are described.

1. Code-breaking practices.

   These practices refer to having access to the skills required to break the code of written texts by recognizing and using fundamental features and architecture, including alphabet, sounds in words, spelling, and structural conventions and patterns.

2. Practices that provide opportunities to participate with text.

   These practices involve participating in understanding and composing meaningful written, visual, and spoken texts, taking into account each text's interior meaning systems in relation to a reader's available knowledge and experiences of other cultural discourses, texts, and meaning systems.

3. Practices for using text.

   These practices involve using texts functionally by knowing about and acting on the different cultural and social functions that various texts perform inside and outside school and understanding that these functions shape the way texts are structured, their tone, their degree of formality, and their sequence of components.

4. Practices that create space for the critical analysis of text.

   These practices involve the critical analysis and transformation of texts by acting on knowledge that texts are not ideologically natural or neutral—that they represent particular points of views while silencing others, and they influence people's ideas—and that their designs and discourses can be critiqued and redesigned in novel and hybrid ways.

Each family of practices is needed for literacy learning, but none in isolation is sufficient. Each of the four is inclusive with each being integral to the achievement of the others.

In the 1970s and 1980s, psycholinguistic and schema theory emphasized reader–text interactions, drawing attention to text-meaning practices or, more specifically, the construction of a reader who used textual and personal resources to coproduce a meaningful reading. In the late 1980s and early 1990s, sociolinguistic and sociosemiotic theory focused attention on language in use during which reading was viewed in terms of what it did, or could accomplish, pragmatically in the real world. Luke and Freebody (1999) assert that reading should be seen as a nonneutral form of cultural practice, one that positions readers in advantageous and disadvantageous ways. They argue that readers need to be able to interrogate the assumptions and ideologies that are embedded in text as well as the assumptions that they, as sociocultural beings, bring to the text. This leads to asking questions such as Whose voice is heard? Who is silenced? Whose reality is presented? Whose reality is ignored? Who is advantaged? Who is disadvantaged? These sorts of questions open spaces for analyzing the discourses or ways of being that maintain certain social practices over others. The Four Resources Model was an important tool for analyzing what sort of literacy practices I was privileging and marginalizing in the classroom. It was clear that teaching from a critical literacy perspective would produce a very different learner who could make more informed decisions in the world. A useful framework for me to think about what kinds of literate beings I want my students to become in the world is Harste's (2001) Halliday Plus Model of Language Learning.

The Halliday Plus Model (see Figure 2) builds on what we already know about language, making use of what has worked and problematizing what hasn't worked. It is based on a belief that literacy is socially constructed and that when different ways of being are made available, literacy can be reconstructed. It begs the questions, What discourses maintain certain social practices? For what purpose? To whose advantage? It also builds on the notion of individuals being multiliterate—that there isn't just one literacy but different literacies that allow different access in a variety of contexts and spaces in the world. In a practical sense, this means that it is not enough for children to learn language, to learn about language, and to learn through language, but that children also need to learn to use language to critique (Harste, 2001). According to Egawa and Harste (2001),

> the ability to sound out words and make meaning from texts makes children good consumers rather than good citizens. To be truly literate, children need to understand how texts work and that they as literate beings have options in terms of how they are going to respond to a particular text in a given setting. (p. 2)

Figure 2. Halliday Plus Model

Learning Language	Learning About Language
Using language and other sign systems as a meaning-making process.	Understanding how texts operate and how they are coded.
Examples of using language to learn. • Read-aloud • Shared reading • Partner reading • Readers Theatre • Independent reading and writing • Writer's notebook • Big Books • Journals • Reading logs	Examples of teaching practices that help students learn about language. • Teaching letter-sound relationships • Comprehension strategies • Minilessons • Demonstrations • Focused lessons • Class charts
Learning Through Language	**Learning to Use Language to Critique**
Using reading and writing as tools and toys for learning about the world.	Using language to question what seems normal and natural as well as to redesign and create alternate social worlds.
Examples of teaching practices that help children to learn through language. • Using text sets • Reflective journals • Literature study • Inquiry or focused study • Sketch to stretch • Process drama	• Social action projects • Building off everyday texts and social issues. • Using texts that provide opportunities for interrogating the word and the world.

From Harste, J.C. (2001). The Halliday Plus Model. In K. Egawa and J.C. Harste, Balancing the literacy curriculum: A new vision. *School Talk*, 7(1), p. 2. Copyright 2001 by the National Council of Teachers of English. Used with permission.

In conversations with other educators regarding the work they do in helping children to understand how texts work, a common denominator has been the use of critical analysis, often referred to as deconstructing text or unpacking text. Less common is what is done *after* the critique, deconstructing, or unpacking. Critical analysis without action seems to keep us in the same place as when we started. In other words, it is the action piece, doing something with what we discover through critical analysis of text, that helps us to participate differently in the world. Hilary Janks was instrumental in helping me to articulate this thinking. She has written about an interdependent model of critical literacy that includes text design or redesign as an essential component of critical literacy work. She notes that central to this work is helping children to understand the relationship between language and power (Janks, 2000), namely that particular discursive practices (ways of talking, doing, being, and acting) carry more or less power or influence in different settings and places. Janks explains that different realizations of critical literacy operate with different conceptions of this relation by foregrounding one orientation or other of domination, access, diversity, or design. Foregrounding one or the other is problematic. For instance, if a curriculum claims to be framed from a difference and diversity perspective but does not simultaneously address issues of dominance, then particular perspectives tend to be privileged while others are marginalized. If this curriculum is not also oriented toward issues of access, then how do we make accessible to our students and help them understand dominant forms that will help them participate differently and more powerfully in the world? Janks argues that these orientations are interdependent. Figure 3 is a representation of my understanding of Janks's model. I use arrows between the circles of domination, access, diversity, and design to show the interconnection between these orientations. At the center is a reminder of the larger sociocultural framework of reading the world as text through which each of the orientations intersect and connect. Circling the orientations are arrows that point clockwise and counterclockwise denoting that there is no sequence or order through which to take up these orientations. Rather, we move fluidly through and between each.

In my teaching, I have for years attempted to create or negotiate class projects with my students that have real-world effects. My book *Negotiating Critical Literacies With Young Children* (Vasquez, 2004) contains several

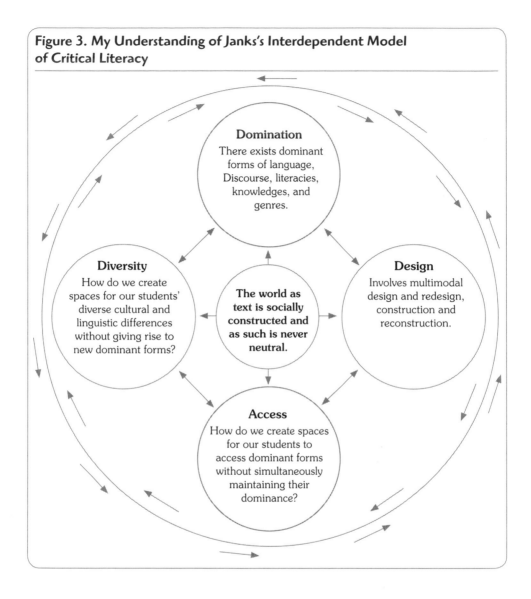

Figure 3. My Understanding of Janks's Interdependent Model of Critical Literacy

Domination
There exists dominant forms of language, Discourse, literacies, knowledges, and genres.

Diversity
How do we create spaces for our students' diverse cultural and linguistic differences without giving rise to new dominant forms?

The world as text is socially constructed and as such is never neutral.

Design
Involves multimodal design and redesign, construction and reconstruction.

Access
How do we create spaces for our students to access dominant forms without simultaneously maintaining their dominance?

examples of what these projects are like in classrooms with very young learners. In Chapter 6 of this book, Kevan Miller does similar work as she and her students embark on a project to create a new weather graph and song for the first-grade classes at their school. I am, therefore, always on the lookout for new ways for students to represent their projects, their thinking, their understandings, and their ideas. This is where the new literacies and new technologies take a place in my theoretical toolkit. Work done in new literacies and new technologies by people like Buckingham and Sefton-Green (1995), Gee (2003), Marsh (2005), and Lankshear and Knobel (2007) have helped me to think through notions of design and redesign and the role these play in creating opportunities to participate in the world differently. In Chapter 8, I go into detail regarding this idea.

How This Book Is Organized

It is important to reemphasize that I use books as only one of many tools for constructing critical literacies, as one of many artifacts for mediating critical literacy work. However, books alone, even those books referred to as social issues texts (Harste, Leland, Lewison, Ociepka, & Vasquez, 2000)—such as texts that address topics of race, class, or gender—are useful as tools to do critical literacy work only insofar as they can be vehicles for discussing issues of power and control. Simply having these books available is not enough. What makes them social issues texts are the differences that the discourses or belief-laden ways of being and talking have on our discussion about those books and the experiences that influence those discussions, along with who is able to participate, in what ways, for what purposes, and to what ends. It is most advantageous to use such books in combination with other texts as a way of helping students to understand that texts are never neutral and that they are constructed for particular reasons and audiences. Using one book and the ideas presented within as a frame through which to read another book provides for a more informed reading than when student are asked to use individual books. Using a combination of multimedia texts (books, songs, everyday texts, etc.) makes for an even more informed reading because this practice relocates meaning making beyond what is gleaned from our experiences with print-based texts, or more specifically books, to sociocultural/sociopolitical spaces.

In the following chapters you will see examples of how books have been paired with other texts, including everyday texts and media reports, to explore various topics and issues. What are central in each of the stories are the issues that the children raise about the world and the difference critical literacy discourse makes in each context. Of importance is what happens when we make available to children more powerful discourses from which to frame discussion about books and everyday life events.

The focus of Chapter 2 is on using everyday texts such as news reports and posters in combination with children's books to engage in social action. I share work I did with kindergarten students as well as work done by David Chiola-Nakai with his sixth-grade students.

In Chapter 3, I talk about Susan Adamson's use of process drama and books written for children as a way to interrogate social inequities in an elementary school where she worked with seven third-grade students. You also read about work done by Janice Shear's fifth-grade students with regard to using a particular children's book in combination with process writing to construct meaning about inequities in their lives.

In Chapter 4, I share work done by Lee Heffernan and her third-grade students as they use a six-step strategy developed by Lee to take up particular social issues such as racism, using what Harste (2003) refers to as "social issues texts" (p. 9).

In Chapter 5, I focus on work done by Michael Muise with fifth- and sixth-grade students when they used a picture book as a springboard for engaging critical literacies in the math curriculum.

In Chapter 6, I bring you into the classroom of Kevan Miller and a group of first-grade students as they redesign everyday texts used as part of the calendar routine in their school. This routine was implemented as part of the science curriculum, and the work Kevan and her students did using the calendar was an opportunity for her to create spaces for critical literacy within that curriculum.

In Chapter 7, I explore the use of everyday issues and texts once more by reflecting on Sarah Vander Zanden and her fifth-grade students' work on rethinking a community practice regarding Arbor Day. This time, however, the critical literacy work done by Sarah and her students took place as part of their social studies curriculum.

In Chapter 8, I take you to Carol Felderman's second-grade classroom where together we created, produced, and made accessible to a worldwide audience a podcast (online broadcast). I share both the process of podcasting as well as the transformative effects of having participated in such an endeavor. I also discuss what I see as a relationship between critical literacy and new technology.

Finally, in the Conclusion I discuss the notion of using language not only to critique but also to rethink and reimagine different, more equitable ways of being in the world as a common element underlying the work outlined in this book.

I have included reflection questions at the end of each chapter as one way for you to connect the ideas in this book with your experiences, and as one way to help you imagine ways of creating spaces for using children's books differently from a critical literacy perspective. This first set of questions is meant to provide a contextual basis for reading the remainder of the book.

I hope that the version of classroom life presented in the following chapters can complement or encourage the vision you have for engaging in powerful ways with texts to create spaces for a more equitably just and fair world for children.

REFLECTION QUESTIONS

1. Obtain a journal in which to write any thoughts, comments, connections, or questions as you read this book. Begin by reflecting on your own experience as a young learner. What kinds of books do you recall reading while you were an elementary school student? In what ways did the books that were made available to you reflect your own experiences? In what ways were the books that were made available to you inconsistent with your own experiences? What were some of the ways that you talked about these books? What purpose did they serve in your life?

2. Make a list of all the children in your classroom, noting their cultural backgrounds. Then walk around the classroom paying close attention to the children's available literature. Write about how closely the books in your classroom reflect the cultural makeup of your students. What can you say about the consistencies or inconsistencies between your students' backgrounds and experiences and the backgrounds and experiences of the characters in the books you make available to those students?

3. Together with your students, make a list of books that you feel should be added to your classroom or school library to ensure that all the children

in the class are reflected in the books available to them. It would be very useful to add to this list throughout the school year.

4. How are you using language in your classroom? Situate your own literacy teaching by noting in what ways you are using language in your classroom using the following four categories: (1) Things that I do to teach language, (2) Things that I do to teach about language, (3) Things that I do to help my students learn through language, and (4) Things that I do to help my students use language to critique.

5. In your journal, reflect on your current theory of language and learning. Begin by naming your theory of language and learning and then write about how what you do in the classroom reflects or is inconsistent with what say you believe. This naming is an important step in rethinking and changing our practice because often our ideologies or beliefs become so much a part of who we are that they become invisible to us. Naming helps to make our theories visible, therefore making these easier for us to reflect and act on more critically.

CHAPTER 2

Pairing Everyday Texts With Texts Written for Children

Curtis:	Who are those again?
Patrick:	Oh, Mounties.
Julia:	When I grow up I can be one!
Roger:	When I grow up I will be a horse.
Emily:	You can't be a horse; you're a person not an animal!
Curtis:	No, you can't! There are no girl Mounties in the poster.

This conversation took place in my kindergarten classroom. The children were referring to a poster of the Royal Canadian Mounted Police (RCMP), which they were using to discuss who could or could not be an RCMP officer. Another student, Jessica, initiated the discussion when she noticed there were no females in the poster. The RCMP, also referred to as Mounties, is Canada's national police force that was founded more than 125 years ago to enforce the law during Canada's early settlement days. Today the RCMP acts as the municipal police force in about 200 Canadian cities and towns.

During the year that this discussion took place, the parents of one of the children in my class were RCMP officers. As such, they were able to arrange for another officer to visit the children. After the visit, the officer left a poster of the Mounties' musical ride team on horseback on a bulletin board in the classroom. On the poster the musical ride team is lined up in a row so the officers' faces are clearly visible. The opening conversation took place as the children began to look closely at the poster while they worked on their various class projects.

Manning (1993) talks about three curricula that play out in the classroom: the mandated curriculum, which is provided by the school district head offices; the paper curriculum, which consists of the curriculum guides that are often part of prepackaged programs; and the real curriculum, which refers to the issues and topics raised by students in classrooms. The conversation at the opening of this chapter represents the real curriculum. Anything that students or teachers bring to the classroom has the potential to become the real curriculum. This curriculum and what children learn from it in terms of skills and content often intersect with the paper and mandated curriculum. It simply looks and sounds different. As the classroom teacher, I took it upon myself to keep track of ways in which this real curriculum complemented or connected with what was required by the school board. What makes the real curriculum sound and look different are the different ways of talking that are brought to bear on the issues raised by children. These different ways of talking, or discourses, provide alternate frameworks through which children can speak about and make meaning in the world around them.

In this chapter, the focus is on the kind of work that can be accomplished when everyday texts are paired with books written for children and what happens when alternate Discourses (Gee, 2005), or ways of being, doing, and talking, are used to engage in discussion about these texts. According to Haas Dyson (2005) everyday texts are as follows:

- Texts that are spoken or written as part of everyday life.

- Texts that are so common that we don't carefully take notice of them.

We are less aware of the kinds of messages about our world that are conveyed by everyday texts. Because these are not natural representations of the world, they can be deconstructed and analyzed to uncover the view of the world they represent to make visible the lifestyles and identities that are constructed through what is presented and through how it is presented. See Table 1 for resources to learn more about everyday texts.

You Can Be a Mountie When You Grow Up

Jessica: There's no girls. There's no girls in it.

Roger: There's men.

Nicholas: 'Cause there's horses.

Table 1. Resources to Learn More About Everyday Texts

Alvermann, D.E., Moon, J.S., & Hagood, M.C. (1999). *Popular culture in the classroom: Teaching and researching critical media literacy.* Newark, DE: International Reading Association; Chicago: National Reading Conference.

Barton, D., & Hamilton, M. (1998). *Local literacies: Reading and writing in one community.* London: Routledge.

Comber, B., Nixon, H., & Reid, J. (2007). (Eds.). *Literacies in place: Teaching environmental communications.* Newtown, NSW, Australia: Primary English Teaching Association.

Comber, B., & Thomson, P. (with Wells, M.). (2001). Critical literacy finds a "place": Writing and social action in a low-income Australian grade 2/3 classroom. *The Elementary School Journal, 101*(4), 451–464.

Marsh, J. (2005). (Ed.). *Popular culture, new media and digital literacy in early childhood.* New York: Routledge Falmer.

O'Brien, J. (1994). Show Mum you love her: Taking a new look at junk mail. *Reading, 28*(1), 43–46.

Vasquez, V. (2000). Building community through social action. *School Talk, 5*(4), 2–3.

Vasquez, V. (2003). What Pokemon can teach us about learning and literacy. *Language Arts, 81*(2), 118–125.

Vasquez, V. (2004). *Negotiating critical literacies with young children.* Mahwah, NJ: Erlbaum.

Vasquez, V. (2007, May). Using the everyday to engage in critical literacies with young children. *New England Reading Association Journal,* pp. 6–11.

Vasquez, V., & Egawa, K. (Eds.). (2002). *Everyday texts, everyday literacies. School Talk, 8*(1), 1–8.

Teacher:	Let's talk about that for a minute. A lot of you have been saying there are no girls in it. What does that tell you? What does this poster say about being a girl Mountie?
Andrea:	Well, um, one time my dad went up a mountain and there was only girls in it. There was no boys.
Teacher:	Oh, really. So there was another—so in that case there were only girls and no boys. Is that what you're saying?
Patrick:	Because there's boys and men and there's no girls because um, girls are not like boys are they?
Teacher:	So do you mean that you don't think they can do this job? That being a Mountie is a boy thing to do? Does anyone have anything they'd like to say about that?

Girls:	Yeah!
Jessica:	Well, my dad. He lets me ride on his back when he's pretending to be a horse to try and catch my brother Kyle. Well, since I know something like I go on my merry-go-round at Woodbine and at Square One [shopping malls], that it tells me that I could go on it too 'cause I know how to ride like girls 'cause both feet on one side and then you ride. But on real horses you gotta hold tight and do the same.
Kyle:	Um, I went on the merry-go-round at Square One and that tells me that um, um, that I like horses and I ride one horse but not with these men on it. I didn't wear the hat like that or the coats.
Andrea:	One time I went on a real horse. My daddy helped me. When I went on the horse I was just 3 years old and I—it was the sister. When she was 4 years old she fell in front of her horsey.
Jessica:	Well, girls, they can take boys' place even if they don't know how to hammer and all that 'cause my mom, dad he works with wood down in the basement to finish it and mom she helps and I'm a girl right? So I help, too. Well, once dad I think was sick, but he didn't tell me the rest 'cause I don't think he was feeling well when he didn't tell me the rest. 'Cause a girl took his place, and he had to get off work 'cause he was starting to bleed or he was sick to get off work.
Teacher:	And a girl took his place?
Jessica:	Yeah.
Teacher:	What do you think about that?
Jessica:	I think that girls could ride horses too!

The Mountie poster, which began a class conversation about how girls/females are constructed by social text, represents one way in which males are privileged in society. If the previous conversation had not taken place, it is possible that this poster would have remained, implicitly stabilizing an inequitable distribution of power between males and females.

The comments made by Andrea, "Well, um, one time my dad went up a mountain and there was only girls in it. There was no boys" and Patrick, "Because there's boys and men and there's no girls because um, girls are not like boys are they?" begin to tease at the students' perception of how boys and girls, and men and women, are positioned by everyday texts such as the poster. Andrea cites an example of an all-girls situation to counter the all-boys Mountie poster. Patrick makes a statement that girls are not like boys, implicitly reasoning that there are no girls in the poster because girls are not like boys. Patrick's statement could lead to the conclusion that girls are not capable of being Mounties because there is something they cannot do that boys are able to do.

As the conversation continued, making problematic the absence of women in the poster, traditional notions of femininity were challenged and traditional male and female roles destabilized. Jessica began to construct her model of possibility for girls and women as she drew from her personal experience of riding horses, "I know something like I go on my merry-go-round at Woodbine and at Square One, that it tells me that I could go on it too 'cause I know how to ride like girls 'cause both feet on one side and then you ride. But on real horses you gotta hold tight and do the same." This was her way of problematizing the absence of females in the Mountie poster, implicitly arguing that girls can ride horses and, therefore, should have been represented in the poster. Jessica made her stance explicit when she declared, "I think that girls could ride horses too!" meaning that females, therefore, also could be Mounties.

In response to this conversation, my students and I searched through our school library for information about the Mounties. One book that the children were most interested in because of the clear, bold illustrations was *The Royal Canadian Mounted Police* written and illustrated by Marc Tetro (1994). The cover of the book depicts a group of five Mounties—some short, others tall, all of them sporting mustaches, all of them male. Immediately, comments were made by both boys and girls in the class regarding this book cover being "just the same" as the poster—they both "mean the same" and "tell us the same." One of the girls asked, "Why?" meaning why do the book cover and poster both exclude women?

While reading the book, another illustration caught the group's attention. The illustration clearly depicted why the Mountie poster was designed as it was—depicting an all-male police force. The text read,

"Among the recruits [RCMP recruits] there were teachers and farmers, students and lumberjacks." All the recruits were male. Some of the children were puzzled by what the text meant but made connections to the poster while looking closely at the illustration. One of the children decided that the person in front must be the farmer because "he is wearing overalls." Someone else decided that a person in the back row must be the student because "the bag he is carrying looks like a backpack." They couldn't decide on which character the lumberjack could be because "what does a lumberjack look like anyway?" They also could not figure out which character the teacher could be because none of them "look like Ms. Vasquez." It was interesting to see the children use their previous experiences—their available cultural capital and ways of being (discourses) that were familiar to them—to construct meaning from the illustrations.

As I continued reading the book, I watched as Andrea and Jessica moved closer to me. "Wait, wait, wait...It's the same again, it's all men and no girls." Women had no part in the history of the RCMP as represented by Tetro's book. I asked them to consider what could have been given to women and girls as responsibilities during the times when the Mounties were first introduced. We looked at some reference books of that time period to see if men were given all the jobs that people thought were important. The children shared examples of women they know who are doctors or lawyers, citing that "Ms. Vasquez is a teacher and she's a girl so it's not exactly the same as before." They were learning that history is a social construction, that previous ways of being can be changed, and that as we live our lives we are in fact writing history.

Picking up on this comment, I shared that there are more jobs taken by women in recent years that have not been available to them in the past. I also shared that this change took a long time and that many women over the years worked hard at making sure that women today have different opportunities. I told them about Emily Stowe, who fought for the rights of women to be admitted to medical school in the 1800s, and Clara Martin, who fought for the rights of women to enter the legal profession. My students and I also talked about how historical constructions, as in the case of the Mounties originally being an all-male group, can easily be maintained and how that might happen. Further discussion took place regarding the need to continue to find ways to make sure that men and women are treated equitably and that women and girls are given the same kinds of opportunities that men are given. Jessica interjected with "and this poster and this book does not make things equal." This comment led to a conversation regarding the need to look critically at the way women and girls are represented in different texts like the poster.

As a class we read other books that presented different ways of being (different positionings) for females. Some of the books included *Mama Is a Miner* (Lyon, 1994), *The Paper Bag Princess* (Munsch, 1988), and *Princess Smartypants* (Cole, 1997). We also read and discussed books in which females were marginalized such as *Counting on Frank* (Clement, 1991) and *Piggybook* (Browne, 1990). All of these books gave us a perspective from which to read magazine fliers and other everyday texts, such as food packaging and toy packaging, and to watch television shows. Recently, many more books have been published that focus on presenting strong female characters. These include books such as *Grace for President* (Dipuchio, 2008), *Julia Morgan Built a Castle* (Mannis, 2006), *Meggie Moon* (Baguley, 2005), *Of Numbers and Stars: The Story of Hypatia* (Love, 2006), and *Sally Jean, the Bicycle Queen* (Best, 2006).

My students and I also talked about doing what we could to help change the way certain groups, such as females, are positioned in society. In response to our conversations, Andrea—whose parents are both in the RCMP—spoke up saying that if they (Mounties) "keep sending this poster out then some people, like girls, won't know that they can be Mounties too."

As our conversation continued, it became clear that, historically, various texts have worked in boys and men. Our conversation implicitly became a way of countering this historical effect and finding ways to have text work differently for girls and women (see Table 2 for books that can be used to create space for discussion on gender issues).

A strategy for extending this conversation is to look through the books you have available in the classroom and list the various roles given to male and female characters. This kind of activity creates space to discuss with children alternate ways of being by having them imagine or rewrite some of the stories to create alternate realities.

Constructing Alternate Realities

Of all the students in the class, Jessica seemed most eager to take action against the inequities discussed in the classroom. She decided that she

Table 2. Children's Books That Can Be Used to Discuss Gender Issues

Breen, S. (2008). *Violet the pilot*. New York: Penguin/Dial Books for Young Readers.

Browne, A. (1986). *Piggybook*. New York: Knopf.

Buehner, C. (1996). *Fanny's dream*. New York: Dial.

Clement, R. (1991). *Counting on Frank*. Milwaukee, WI: Gareth Stevens.

Cole, B. (1997). *Princess Smartypants*. New York: Putnam.

dePaola, T. (1979). *Oliver Button is a sissy*. San Diego, CA: Harcourt Brace Jovanovich.

Fitzgerald, D. (2005). *Getting in the game*. New York: Roaring Brook.

Henson, H. (2008). *That book woman*. New York: Simon & Schuster.

Hoffman, M. (1991). *Amazing Grace*. New York: Dial.

Hopkinson, D. (2001). *Under the quilt of night*. New York: Atheneum.

Karr, K. (2005). *Mama went to jail for the vote*. New York: Hyperion Books for Children.

Kessler, C. (2000). *My great-grandmother's gourd*. New York: Orchard.

Kessler, C. (2006). *The best beekeeper of Lalibela: A tale from Africa*. New York: Holiday House.

Lipp, F. (2001). *The caged birds of Phnom Penh*. New York: Holiday House.

Lipp, F. (2008). *Running shoes*. Watertown, MA: Charlesbridge.

Lyon, G. (1994). *Mama is a miner*. New York: Scholastic.

Mackall, D.D. (2008). *A girl named Dan*. Farmington Hills, MI: Sleeping Bear.

Maury, I. (1976). *My mother the mail carrier/Mi mamá la cartera*. New York: Feminist Press.

McCully, E.A. (1996). *The bobbin girl*. New York: Dial.

McCully, E.A. (2000). *Mirette & Bellini cross Niagara Falls*. New York: Putnam.

Miller, W. (1994). *Zora Hurston and the chinaberry tree*. New York: Lee & Low.

Munsch, R. (1986). *The paper bag princess*. Toronto, ON: Annick.

Pinkney, A.D. (2000). *Let it shine: Stories of black women freedom fighters*. San Diego, CA: Harcourt.

Pinkney, A.D. (2003). *Fishing day*. New York: Hyperion.

Schroeder, A. (2000). *Minty: A story of young Harriet Tubman*. New York: Puffin.

Sills, L. (2005). *From rags to riches: A history of girls' clothing in America*. New York: Holiday House.

Yolen, J. (2002). *Hippolyta and the curse of the Amazons*. New York: HarperCollins.

Zipes, J. (Ed.). (1989). *Don't bet on the prince: Contemporary feminist fairy tales in North America and England*. New York: Routledge Kegan & Paul.

Zolotow, C. (1972). *William's doll*. New York: Harper & Row.

needed to show the Mounties what the poster should look like today, "because today, women are Mounties also." In other words, women should not only be given the opportunity to become RCMP but, in fact, they already are in position as RCMP officers; therefore, their presence should be recognized. She called her poster "My Poster of the Way the Mountie Poster Should Be" (see Figure 4). In Jessica's poster there is an equitable number of men and women represented. Once completed, she asked me to help her with a letter to the Mounties (see Figure 5). Jessica decided to send both the letter and the poster to the RCMP office in the city where she lived.

A few weeks after having posted her letter and poster, the father of one of the children in another class, who was a RCMP officer, approached

Figure 4. Jessica's Mountie Poster

Figure 5. Jessica's Letter

The letter reads,
Could you please change the poster because there are girls in the Mounties (police force).

me and asked if someone from my class had sent a letter to the RCMP. He then proceeded to share that no one had ever pointed out the inequity in the poster before. When I asked what action would be taken as a result of Jessica's letter, he replied by saying that if those in charge of media promotions do not do anything to resolve this issue that the women in his department certainly would. This Mountie story became a metaphor for the way in which my students and I read different texts in our classroom. This included everyday texts such as the Mountie poster and books written for children. No longer did the children read blindly, accepting how texts construct them; they began to realize how text could be reconstructed in more equitable ways not only for boys and girls and men and women, but also for people or groups who have been marginalized, disadvantaged, or discriminated against.

In the next section of this chapter, you will meet David Chiola-Nakai and his class of 32 sixth-grade students in a Catholic school in the greater Toronto area of Ontario, Canada, and hear about ways that they used everyday text along with text written for children as one way to create space for critical literacy.

Pairing Media Texts With Texts Written for Children

Teacher:	What are the "uniforms" that kids wear in school?
Victor:	What do you mean?
Teacher:	Well, what kinds of clothes do cool kids wear? How do we know when someone is "cool"?
Tomislav:	Cool kids wear Nike.
Others:	Nike is the best. Yeah! Nike rules!

Like my kindergarten students and me, David Chiola-Nakai and his sixth-grade students also worked with everyday texts in combination with books written for children. The above conversation was part of a discussion following a read-aloud of *The Hockey Story* by R.J. Childerhose (1981). The story is about a hockey game between a team from an urban area and one from a rural area. David's students were immediately drawn to the obvious difference between the two teams' uniforms. The team from the city wore matching uniforms and was outfitted from helmet to skates.

The team from the rural area wore a ragtag mix of whatever equipment and uniforms they could find. This contrast in the resources available to each team led David, together with his students, to discuss inequity and the ways that people can position one another in classist ways, including judging someone based on the clothes he or she wears. As part of that conversation, they discussed what clothing is considered "cool" and wondered who determines what is cool. The preceding conversation took place as part of the discussion on this topic.

Bigelow, Christensen, Karp, Miner, and Peterson (1994) state "if we ask students to critique the world but then fail to encourage them to act, our classrooms can degenerate into factories for cynicism" (p. 4). In other words, to critique void of action does not lead to change. The only thing it can lead to is the creation of cynics who talk about what is wrong with the world without contributing to changing that world. David recognized that he could capitalize on his students' interest in Nike to engage in critical literacy that could lead to some sort of social action. The following exchange took place even before he could begin to address the notion of taking action in the world to change inequitable ways of being.

> Tomislav: But Nike is all over the world. How can we make a change?
>
> Victor: We could stop buying their products.
>
> Mike: I'll never stop buying Nike!

It became clear to David that engaging in critical literacy work could cause tension in the classroom. Some of his students were clearly expressing anticorporate agenda sentiments, while others treasured the cultural capital that came with being a Nike wearer.

Finding comfort in the notion that tension is a great propeller of learning, David forged on regardless of the tensions he began to face regarding how to enact a critical curriculum.

A Nike Story: Using Tensions to Propel Learning

A social system can only be held in place by the meanings the people make of it. Culture is deeply inscribed in the differential distribution of power within a society, for power relations can only be stabilized or destabilized by the meanings that

33

people make of them. Culture is a struggle for meanings as society is a struggle for power. (Fiske, 1989, p. 20)

According to Fiske (1989), a social system or a society's accepted ways of being are maintained through use. The important question is, Who decides on what systems to maintain and use and for what purposes? Who gets to do what, however, is rooted in who has or does not have power to act in particular ways. Fiske refers to this as a differential distribution of power.

David wondered how Fiske's notion of the differential distribution of power intersected with the issue of classism and inequity his students had raised. He realized that not acting on these issues in some way or at least making visible to his students possible ways of taking action would mean that he and his students would be contributing to maintaining inequitable ways of being.

While attempting to figure out how to deal with his students' struggle for meaning, David mentioned their conversation regarding Nike to one of his colleagues, who proceeded to tell him about a television report on Nike's mistreatment of factory workers in developing countries. In response, David asked if she would talk to his class and share what she had seen. At that time, he had not realized the generative nature of connecting everyday text such as the television segment with the original conversations regarding equity in *The Hockey Story* (Childerhose, 1981).

> David: I began to sense my students' growing awareness of the overwhelming presence Nike had in their lives. They began to take much more notice of the plethora of Nike gear worn in the school. I heard disbelief in their voices as they began to discuss issues of fair wages and child labor and the role that we play as consumers in maintaining children as laborers when we consume Nike products. Posters appeared on the classroom walls depicting anti-Nike sentiments. Similar to the way it has come to dominate the sports world, the Nike sports empire suddenly became the focus of a classroom study.
>
> I could feel the sense of being overwhelmed by the idea of taking on such a huge conglomerate. Imagine a group of 11- to 12-year-old students taking on the giant of the sports world. But as Harste (1997) has said, history is replete with examples of "tripping the giant" (p. 2).

What started as a conversation about a children's book turned into a discussion around issues of power and consumerism when the issues raised in the book were paired with the inequities made visible in a television segment.

Creating Spaces for Students to Think Differently

David: I started to see how the classroom could offer space for analyzing the daily texts that students bring to school. I realized that spaces for conversation on social issues could come from an assortment of texts, not just books. I think I was beginning to further my understanding of interrogating texts and how to make them problematic. I could also see how the classroom was becoming a safe zone for my students to critically analyze the world around them. Not everyone took the same position. Many remained loyal to Nike and refused to stop wearing the brand name's clothing or shoes. Others engaged in a personal boycott, stripping their bodies of any sort of Nike wear to symbolize their protest against the corporation's treatment of their workers.

David found himself caught in the whirlwind of events happening in and out of the classroom. His role became blurred as he found himself in the position of both a resource and a learner. He searched the papers and magazines to provide articles and materials to support his students' inquiries and found new ways of using existing learning tools and strategies (see Table 3 for resources on media literacy).

Table 3. Resources on Media Literacy

Alvermann, D.E., Moon, J.S., & Hagood, M.C. (1999). *Popular culture in the classroom: Teaching and researching critical media literacy.* Newark, DE: International Reading Association; Chicago: National Reading Conference.

Buckingham, D. (1993). *Children talking television: The making of television literacy.* London: Routledge Falmer.

Buckingham, D., & Sefton-Green, J. (1995). *Cultural studies goes to school: Reading and teaching popular media.* London: Taylor & Francis.

Evans, J (2005). *Literacy moves on: Popular culture, new technologies, and critical literacy in the elementary classroom.* Portsmouth, NH: Heinemann.

Gee, J.P. (2003). *What video games have to teach us about learning and literacy.* New York: Palgrave Macmillan.

Kavanagh, K. (1997). *Texts on television: School literacies through viewing in the first years of school.* Adelaide, South Australia: Department of Education and Children's Services.

Klein, N. (2000). *No logo: Taking aim at the brand bullies.* Toronto, ON: Vintage Canada.

Lankshear, C., & Knobel, M. (2007). *A new literacies sampler.* New York: Peter Lang.

Marsh, J. (2005). (Ed.) *Popular culture, new media and digital literacy in early childhood.* New York: Routledge Falmer.

David: I began to see how we could use surveys and graphing, investigating maps and charts, money, letter writing, learning logs, posters, questionnaires, response logs, and presentations in our investigations. For example, two students designed a survey to find out the approximate number of hats, shoes, and shirts that were owned by students in our school and how many of these were Nike products. They took the information and drew graphs and reported what they had discovered to the rest of the class to show the predominance of Nike consumers. They then went on to do a presentation to our reading buddies, first-grade students with whom we read picture books once a week, about Nike's mistreatment of workers. I found this helped my students to articulate their concerns better while disseminating information they thought was important.

Many students designed posters depicting anti-Nike sentiment. These were alternate versions of existing Nike ads. Two other students wrote a joint letter to Phillip Knight, CEO of Nike, asking him to tell Nike's side of the story on the use of child laborers and the use of sweatshops.

Comber (2001) notes,

Children are accustomed to thinking analytically about power and pleasure....
The task for teachers is to help children to develop a meta-awareness and a meta-language for what they already know how to do and to assist them in applying these resources to the texts and situations of school life. The varying practices that different children bring with them can become part of a collective capacity to solve problems and approach possibilities. (p. 2)

Developing a collective capacity to solve problems and approach possibilities is one of the goals that David had hoped could be accomplished through the class inquiry. The point of the inquiry was not to make people change their minds but to provide students with new ways of talking and thinking about "the everyday worlds of community, media, and literature" (Comber, 2001, p. 2) to make informed critical decisions.

Reading text sets (see Table 4 for resources on text sets) on a particular topic can help students to understand that texts are never neutral, and that they are constructed by particular people with particular goals and motivations (Comber, 2001). A text set is a group of books and other print and media materials such as magazine articles and video clips designed to support the study of a particular theme, genre, or issue. A set usually consists of at least four or five texts and should be carefully constructed to provide different perspectives. Sometimes these perspectives are complementary and other times they may be conflicting, but nevertheless they offer a way of viewing the same area under study. In the case of the

Table 4. Resources to Learn More About Text Sets

Harste, J.C., Leland, C., Lewison, M., Ociepka, A., & Vasquez, V. (2000). Supporting critical conversations in classrooms. In K.M. Pierce (Ed.), *Adventuring with books: A booklist for Pre-K–Grade 6* (12th ed., pp. 507–512). Urbana, IL: National Council of Teachers of English.

Leland, C., Harste, J.C., Ociepka, A., Lewison, M., & Vasquez, V. (1999). Exploring critical literacy: You can hear a pin drop. *Language Arts, 77*(1), 70–77.

Short, K.G., Harste, J.C., & Burke, C.L. (1996). *Creating classrooms for authors and inquirers.* Portsmouth, NH: Heinemann

Nike inquiry, David's students learned to read between the lines of Nike ads as well as media reports on Nike's corporate practices, which all started from the inequities that his students noticed in a story about a hockey game.

In this chapter, David and I demonstrated how we paired children's books with everyday texts to develop social action projects with our students. Our hope was for our experiences to make visible the potential for learners to live critically literate lives regardless of age. My students were only 4 years old when they took on the Mountie poster as text. David's students were 11 and 12 years old. Both groups of learners, however, worked equally as hard at attempting to engage critical literacies in their own settings in an attempt to change inequitable ways of being. As a result of these experiences, as classroom teachers, David and I learned what it means for students to take social action as a result of using a critical literacy perspective in the classroom. It also became clear to us that this kind of work is not about telling people what to think or how to think but about giving them opportunities to ponder and discuss social issues that matter in their lives from different perspectives. In the next chapter, you will meet Susan Adamson and Janice Shear as together with their students they explore ways of using children's literature to make meaning from social issues that take place in their respective school communities.

REFLECTION QUESTIONS

1. Make a list of everyday texts you can find in your community along with the everyday texts your students bring to the classroom (magazines, ads,

posters and cards, T-shirt logos, logos on backpacks, lunch bags, and so forth). How might you use these materials in combination with children's books to create curricular activities and materials?

2. Linger with one of the everyday texts that you found. How might you support your students to redesign problematic notions of the text? How might you design an alternate version from a different, more equitable perspective?

3. Together with your students, look closely at the books in your classroom or library. Survey what roles males and females are assigned in the books and how many times each of these roles appears in the books. Look closely at your survey results. Who is assigned roles of power or more powerful roles? Who is assigned less powerful roles? Are these roles consistent with the roles taken on by males and females in your community? What are some ideas for rewriting the storylines in some of the books toward more equitable gender representation?

CHAPTER 3

Using Children's Literature to Unpack Social Issues in the School Community

Lauren:	They're just watching!
Teacher:	Why are they just watching?
Chase:	Because they don't care what happens to black people.
Teacher:	What do you think? If you saw this out in the street, what would you want to do?
Ethan:	I'd kick their butt.
Melissa:	I'd call the police.
Tommy:	I'd beat them up and run.
Teacher:	You have to think of your own safety too, right?
Melissa:	They might have guns.
Ethan:	But what if they do have guns, you never know.
Chase:	Trip them and knock them out. Then say, "Who got the gun now?"
Teacher:	I'm asking you what you are able to do. You might want to go over there and beat them up, but you can't do that because you will probably get hurt.
Lauren:	But when someone's fighting like that you should go over there and help them.
Teacher:	How can you help? What can you do?
Sean:	Call the police!
Tommy:	You can talk them out of it.
Emily:	OK, pretend I have a gun and I'm about to shoot you. What are you going to do? Talk me out of it. Talk me out

of it. (She points her finger at Tommy like it's a gun.) I'm crazy. I'm drunk. Talk me out of it. I'm the one with the gun. Talk me out of it.

T his exchange marked a critical moment in Susan Adamson's work with a group of third graders as they focused on making sense of the world through interrogating and analyzing picture books in light of their own experiences. In this chapter you will meet Susan as well as Janice Shear and her fifth graders. Both Susan and Janice struggled with what to do with topics related to issues of power and control in their respective classrooms. (See Table 5 for a list of books that can be used to create space to talk about issues of racism, power, and control.)

White Wash: Taking Up Issues of Power and Control in the Classroom

The conversation at the start of this chapter stemmed from a read aloud of the picture book *White Wash* (Shange, 1997). The story centers on a young African American girl, Helene-Angel, who is traumatized when

---

Table 5. Books for Creating Space to Talk About Racism, Power, and Control

Bunting, E. (1998). *So far from the sea*. New York: Clarion.

Coleman, E. (1996). *White socks only*. Morton Grove, IL: Albert Whitman.

Hubbard, J. (1996). *Lives turned upside down: Homeless children in their own words and photographs*. New York: Simon & Schuster.

Lester, J. (1998). *From slave ship to Freedom Road*. New York: Puffin.

Lorbiecki, M. (1996). *Just one flick of a finger*. New York: Dial.

Riggio, A. (1997). *Secret signs: Along the Underground Railroad*. Honesdale, PA: Boyds Mill Press.

Russell, E. (2000). *A is for Aunty*. New South Wales, Australia: ABC Books.

Tunnell, M.O., & Chilcoat, G.W. (1996). *The children of Topaz: The story of a Japanese American internment camp*. New York: Holiday House.

Weatherford, C.B. (2005). *Freedom on the menu: The Greensboro sit-ins*. New York: Dial Books for Young Readers.

Winslow, V. (1997). *Follow the leader*. New York: Delacorte.

a gang attacks her and her brother, Mauricio, on their way home from school. During the attack the gang members spray paint the little girl's face white, telling her they were doing her a good deed teaching her how to be white, teaching her how to be American. While reflecting on the children's conversation, Susan noted,

> The children struggled with their sense of individual power and significance in relationship to their world. Their outrage was potent, a palpable strength of their knowing, but they were rendered impotent as no reasonable course of action occurred to them. Undaunted they continued to explore a repertoire of actions using their own personal text to guide them.

In what ways can children's books be used to create space for children to work through struggles regarding issues of power in their local settings? What kinds of strategies might classroom teachers put in place to help them make sense of that world? How might children use the texts of their everyday lives to read children's books? These are a few of the questions asked by Susan while she worked with a group of 7 third-graders in an urban public school in a midwestern U.S. town. Her reflection deals with her students' responses to the book and the difficulty they experienced when making sense of the racism presented in the text. Observing their emotional reaction to the text and seeing the children animate their bodies in response by moving around the space they occupied and motioning with their arms and hands, Susan decided to use process drama to take up issues of power and control in the book. The result was engaging in social action at their school site to specifically address racism and violence on the playground.

Acting Out: Using Process Drama to Read Critically

In her reflection, Susan commented on how the children undauntedly continued to explore their repertoire of possible actions. The children's repertoire of actions included using process drama as a way of constructing meaning and unpacking text. In this case, they unpack White Wash (Shange, 1997). I deliberately chose not to focus on methods for engaging in process drama in this section as this is not my intent with this chapter. However, Table 6 contains resources regarding this process. Instead, my intent is to demonstrate one way in which students can draw from their

Table 6. Resources on Process Drama

Cowan, K., & Albers, P. (2006). Semiotic representations: Building complex literacy practices through the arts. *The Reading Teacher, 60*(2), 124–137. doi:10.1598/RT.60.2.3

Fennessey, S. (2006). Using theater games to enhance language arts learning. *The Reading Teacher, 59*(7), 688–691. doi:10.1598/RT.59.7.7

Schneider, J.J., Crumpler, T.P., & Rogers, T. (2006). *Process drama and multiple literacies: Addressing social, cultural, and ethical issues.* Portsmouth, NH: Heinemann.

Schneider, J.J., & Jackson, S.A.W. (2000). Process drama: A special space and place for writing. *The Reading Teacher, 54*(1), 38–51.

past experiences—in this case what they already knew about "acting out" scenarios—to make sense of new experiences. What is most interesting about Susan's work, as described in this chapter, is her venture into process drama as a tool to help her students use the book *White Wash* to address issues of violence and racism.

The opening discussion took place after Susan read *White Wash* to her group. Susan noted how the children overtly struggled with their sense of individual power and significance during the conversation. The conversation continued:

Ethan:	Scream bloody murder.
Melissa:	Say "fire." "Fire!" That's what my Mom says to do.
Chase:	That's what my Mom says, too. Even if they have a gun and tells you not to scream. You scream.
Emily:	What if they have a knife?
Teacher:	That's a really big dilemma because you have to decide whether to scream, and if you do they might harm you.

The children felt an urge to act out this scenario. They had already started to do this when Emily pretended to have a gun and asked Tommy to "Talk me out of it." At first their dramatizations seemed futile as they ultimately dissolved into laughter.

Susan: At this point Emily had assigned parts to the other students. While she played the part of "herself," she assigned two of the other boys to be her younger brothers and asked Tommy to be the "guy with the knife." Rather than situate them on the street as the children were in the story, her scenario had them in her house in one of the upstairs bedrooms. On her cue, the "brothers" began to cower in the corner while she tried to confront Tommy. As he slinked over, though, with his arm extended as if holding a knife, they all dissolved into laughter, falling on the floor or collapsing in a chair. But they quickly regrouped, clamoring to try new parts; "Let me try, let me try" they shouted, as if they were more up to the task than the others were. At each attempt (two or three more), laughter prevailed.

In spite of the laughter, the potential of using process drama to make explicit the children's tensions and anxieties was clear. While reflecting on this experience after the fact, Susan realized that the laughter reflected the children's anxiety with playing roles that had not been part of their schema. Previously they had used drama to act out scenes from books, as they appeared, but not as a way to problem solve to construct new meaning. She noted that adding to the children's discomfort was their own sense of powerlessness in being unable to figure what to do when faced with such danger. Process drama provided an opportunity to represent the issues they struggled with using an alternate sign system that helped them act out the complexity of the issue at hand.

In response, Susan decided to propose an alternative. She wanted her students to be able to think more explicitly about their own feelings in relation to the inequalities of which they have direct experience (Epstein, 1993; Heffernan & Lewison, 2000). They examined more closely the micropolitics of the playground in their school where they found similar dilemmas, against the backdrop of their own lives. At the school, students relied on teachers to mediate conflicts but often found them to be unfair, ineffective, or unresponsive. This led to a study of behavior on the playground in which Susan and her seven students discussed their observations of negative interactions during recess. They were disturbed by what they saw. Acting on their belief that playground supervision needed to be revisited, they initiated a letter-writing campaign informing the principal of what they deemed to be a crisis in the playground.

Luke and Freebody (1997) write that students bring to the classroom available cultural, community, and social resources, and texts and discourses. Said differently, all students come to school with cultural and social experiences and particular ways of saying and doing things. These various experiences, or cultural and linguistic resources, connect in multiple ways. What this means is learning environments need to be responsive to the cultural discourses that students have access to and are active in, by looking closely at the things that are important to them or that they feel have importance in their lives.

> Susan: The books we read and the conversations we had about those books made the cultural texts of the children I worked with easy to access. The books generated rich discussion of issues such as power, ageism, race, and gender. The students were comfortable expressing their ideas verbally; they appeared to speak openly and honestly. As such, our critical conversations offered several possible insights into how they were negotiating issues of social justice.

According to Susan, in the third-grade classroom there was no shortage of opportunities to engage in important conversations about social justice and equity issues that stemmed from her students' lived experiences. It was simply a matter of determining which conversations to pursue. Susan notes that as teachers we must keep in mind Epstein's (1993) notion of children as active in the construction of their own realities and subjectivities and, therefore, potentially active in the deconstruction of dominant ideologies. Dominant ideologies refer to prevalent societal beliefs. These ideologies are socially constructed; that is, they are created through social interactions between and among people. As such, they can be deconstructed and reconstructed.

> Susan: There are clearly many complicating factors in the construction of meaningful ideologies, but giving credence to one's own experience would seem crucial to empowerment and lead to the deconstruction of dominant ideologies. This is at least part of what I understand critical literacy intends to do.
>
> The cultural climate of this school has yet to challenge these students to analyze their beliefs in a way that lets them create their own well-considered belief systems. They were articulate and empathetic regarding issues of social justice and equity, and they saw a flawed system in which their counterpart, the adult, did not always support them. So while they seemed predisposed to act, they were not able to do so because there was no "space" for social action and, therefore, no space for the creation of alternative ideologies. But given the opportunity, these children would surely find their voices. And given their voices, we surely must listen.

One way to help create space for conversations that may lead to social action is by making accessible to children books that lend themselves more readily to discussions regarding issues of social justice and equity. Harste and colleagues (2000, p. 507) created a set of criteria that is useful for choosing such books:

- They don't make difference invisible, but rather explore what differences make a difference.
- They explore dominant systems of meaning that operate in our society to position people in particular ways.
- They create space for taking action on important social issues.
- They help us to unpack our understanding of history by giving us an opportunity to hear from those who have been traditionally silenced or marginalized.
- They help us to question why certain groups are positioned as "other."

Writing Out: Using Writing to Read Critically

After reading Toni and Slade Morrison's (Morrison & Morrison, 1999) *The Big Box*, Janice Shear's fifth-grade gifted students in Mississauga, Ontario, Canada, expressed sentiments similar to Susan's students with regard to social systems that they felt take freedom away from children.

The book has a haunting message about children who fall outside socially accepted norms. In poetic form, the authors tell the stories of Patty, Mickey, and Lisa Sue who live in a big brown box with doors that open only one way. The adults responsible for these children felt that their behavior required they be locked away because they are unable to handle their freedom. While reflecting on her students' initial reaction to the book, Janice wrote,

> As I closed the book there was an audible sigh from the class. The kids, blinking at each other as if newly awakened from a dream, started some quiet talk, which quickly picked up momentum. The spell had been broken, reality reentered, ideas surfaced. They talked among themselves and repeatedly chanted a line from the book, "They just can't handle their freedom."
>
> They asked me to read the book again. This time they anticipated my reading of the line, chanting repeatedly as I read on.

After first reading *The Big Box* aloud to her class, Janice described her students' being delighted with the line "they just can't handle their freedom" as somewhat problematic. She felt that they did not take the book seriously. Nevertheless, Janice persisted in discussing the book further, and when they did the tone of the children's conversation changed.

> Janice: After the second reading of the book, [the students] were really upset as to why the characters were placed in the big box. They expressed feelings of anger at the parents and other adults who were responsible and were genuinely puzzled as to what regarding the children's behaviors led their parents to believe that they couldn't handle their freedom. They expressed concern with some adults and institutions that do not allow people to be themselves but realized that when someone is different they are sometimes picked on and in a sense "boxed."

The notion of being "boxed" or "othered" led Janice's students to consider what boxes meant in their own lives. They made statements such as "The box is a place to put a problem so you don't have to deal with it" and "It is a mental [in your head] place rather than a physical place." The box they most identified with was being misunderstood by other students or by adults. To make further sense of their discussions, Janice asked her students to write in their journals about their thoughts regarding the book and the notion of being boxed. These were reflective pieces that were informally written with the intent of providing a space for the children to articulate their thinking and their feeling. Another strategy for helping children to articulate their thinking is 3 Plusses and a Wish (Burke, 1997), whereby students are asked to write about three things they connected with in the text and one question that came to mind as they read the text or one wish for how they might have wanted the text to unfold. What's on your mind? is another strategy developed by Burke (1997). With this strategy, students are asked to comment in general or specifically about the text and pose comments, connections, or questions that came to mind as they read the text. Reading With a Post-It is another useful strategy that I have seen used by Rise Paynter in her fifth-grade classroom in Bloomington, Indiana. Rise had her students jot down words or ideas on sticky notes, which they then affixed to the pages of the text they were reading. The children would then return to these sticky notes when discussing the texts with their classmates or during class discussion.

Janice's students commented that writing their thoughts helped them to organize their thinking about the text. It seemed writing was a way for Janice's students to think critically about *The Big Box*. While talking about his writing, Kyle described the box as a mental prison. He said,

It doesn't really exist. The parents made the big box up to trap the kids. And if it was real, it works like a playpen. It traps the kids inside, but the parents, teachers, etc., have complete access to them.

Liane connected with being boxed in as a result of being labeled as gifted. She reflected,

> The other time I've been in a box was when my old friends officially knew I was gifted and they made something up called Liane Carrabanna. They said this character went to St. Rose and they hated her. It was very weird because they were always telling me about her, so I suspected something. I knew it was me. I was right. It was me. It was OK at first, but then I asked them why. They said they did it because I was too smart for them. I think the one way everyone puts everyone else in a box is when we don't give them chances and choices.

Katherine connected to having been boxed in as a result of being female:

> I've been put in a box a couple of times in my life, like when I get grounded. When people (especially boys my age or a bit older) say I'm substitute in a soccer game, or I'm sitting on the bench for the whole game because I'm "only a girl" because they (the team) don't need a girl.

After listening to her students' responses and reflecting on her own journal entries, Janice revisited her concern regarding their initial reaction to the book. She said, "Looking back, it seems to me that they needed to have some fun with the book to offset the intensity of their reactions."

Until Janice talked further with her students, she had not considered the multiplicity of issues regarding gender equity, fairness, and social justice that her students were mulling over in their minds. It was not until she read their writing and listened to their responses that she began to recognize these issues as important ones to take up in the classroom. Like Susan, Janice was not prepared for how her students might react to tensions that were clearly new to them. However, both realized that reading and responding critically could not be a one-time experience. As each of them dealt with the social issues that began to surface in their own settings, they noticed other issues beginning to emerge. For example, in Katherine's writing about *The Big Box*, it became clear to Janice that gender equity was an issue that she ought to take up in the classroom. In Susan's class, the issue of white privilege emerged as her students raised concern over why some white characters in *White Wash* (Shange, 1997) "just watched" without consequence as young Helene-Angel's face was painted white. The important lesson to be gained from this chapter, therefore, is that there is no one-size-fits-all critical literacy, and that we need to construct different critical literacies depending on what work needs to be done in certain settings, contexts, or communities, and that it needs to be negotiated using the cultural and linguistic resources to which children have had access.

A Multimedia Text Set on Issues of Power and Control

In Chapter 2, I talked about using text sets as a powerful way to help children to understand that texts are never neutral and that they are always created from particular perspectives to convey certain messages. Text sets I have seen used in classrooms consist primarily of children's picture books or a combination of picture and chapter books. Even more powerful is to create multimedia text sets. This would include texts created using other sign systems such as paintings, sculptures, movies, and music. A sign system is a way of representing meaning using different materials (media such as paint and clay) and ways of communicating (media such as a painting, video, or sculpture). Each text in the set can be used to read the others in the text. For instance, as a way of better understanding or talking about the issues in *White Wash* (Shange, 1997), the book could be paired with other texts that reflect similar issues. One text can then be used as a lens, framework, or perspective to read the other.

For example, art work created by artists from the stolen generation of Australia would certainly enrich the conversation on power, control, identity, and positioning reflected in the work done by both Susan and Janice's students. The "stolen generation" refers to the Aboriginal people of Australia who were taken from their families as young children to breed the Aborigine out of them. In essence, this was a way to make them white as was the case with the racial incident experienced by Helene-Angel. Pamela Croft, an Aboriginal Australian artist, is part of the stolen generation. According to Sheila M. Poole (2004) of *The Atlanta Journal-Constitution*, who wrote about Croft, "From 1870 to 1970, Australia's government instituted a policy to erase Aboriginal culture. An estimated 100,000 Aboriginal and Torres Strait Islander children were forcibly removed from their homes and adopted by white families or sent to orphanages" (p. 49). Poole states that the plan called for the Aboriginal people to fully assimilate into the white community. Often this assimilation resulted in their role as domestic servants and laborers. Individuals and groups who were part of the stolen generation have since begun to create various kinds of texts, as a way of remembering and as a way of rising up from their oppressive experience. Matt Ruggles, director of *Back to Brisbane*, a documentary on Croft's life, shared with me that Pamela's story as a child of the stolen generation is tragic yet inspirational (personal communication, May 9, 2009). He notes that Croft is an advocate of working toward making the future better for future generations. *Back to Brisbane* is about Croft finding and claiming her identity as an Aboriginal person who uses art for healing, education, and making social and political statements to contribute to change. (For more on *Back to Brisbane* by 7th Wave Pictures, go to www.backtobrisbane.com.) An example of her work is the mural she created in Atlanta, Georgia, United States. The art piece, which is a 20-foot-tall, 100-foot-wide mural called "Bringing Nations, Cultures and Communities Together," according to Poole (2004), may be the largest example of Aboriginal art in the world (see Figure 6A and 6B for a photo of Croft and a partial look at her mural). The handprints represent connecting the human spirit with Mother Earth. The blue lines symbolize rivers. These lines run across the entire mural. A map of Australia is painted in another section of the mural in the Aboriginal colors of red, black, and yellow. There's the wildlife of Australia—a kangaroo, goanna lizard, emu, and platypus. Croft created the mural on the side of the Australian Bakery Cafe on Flat Shoals Avenue, in Atlanta, Georgia, to thank the people of the city for being so good to her son, David, who lived in the area, as well as to give the Australian community there an ambience of home. "Symbols identify who you are," said Croft. "It shows you belong to a place. I did it for my future generations" (as cited in Poole, 2004, p. 49). The future for Croft was not so certain a few decades ago. Today she is known as Dr. Pamela Croft-Warcon, Australia's first indigenous person to gain a doctorate in visual art.

Imagine then how powerful it would be to use *White Wash* and Croft's art as a way of talking about issues of identity, power, and control. Other

texts that can be used alongside these two texts are a Stolen Generation Timeline (see Figure 7) and a clip from the movie *Back to Brisbane* (Figure 8). Older children could even read The Northern Territory of Australia Aboriginal Ordinance 1918, which resulted in Aboriginal children being taken from their families and placed on special reserves. An image of the primary document of this ordinance can be viewed at the National Library of Australia website (nla.gov.au/nla.aus-vn1949075-2x). Not only would this combination of multimedia texts provide spaces for rich discussion but they also demonstrate ways in which the children could represent their thinking. (For other examples of multimedia text sets refer to Table 7.)

In the next chapter, you will continue to hear about other ways of taking up critical literacies in the classroom. This time you will meet Lee Heffernan, who focuses on social issues by bringing the outside world into the classroom.

Figure 7. The Stolen Generation Timeline

- 1937: Aboriginal people are required to be assimilated into white culture. Separate education facilities are set up by the government and Aboriginal children are taken from their families and placed on special reserves.
- 1967: In a vote to alter the constitution, the Australian government is given the power to make laws on Aboriginal affairs.
- 1995: The government has a national inquiry into the forcible removal of Aboriginal children from their homes between 1870 and 1970. The report concludes that the government had knowingly pursued a policy of genocide in regard to the Aboriginal peoples.
- 1997: The "Bringing Them Home Report" reveals the extent of forced removal and its consequences.
- 1999: On May 26, Australia holds its first "Sorry Day" as a public apology to the Aboriginal population for their suffering.
- 2000: Aboriginal athlete and eventual 400 meters gold medalist Cathy Freeman represents Australia in the Sydney Olympics.
- 2001: The Australian census lists 410,000 of its 18,769,249 population as being "Indigenous." Of that number, 366,429 are listed as "Aboriginal."

Information from Zeccola, J. (2001). *Human Rights and Equal Opportunity Commission Report.* Australian Bureau of Statistics 2001 Census.

Figure 8. Back to Brisbane

Table 7. Examples of Multimedia Text Sets

Acts of Courage and Acts of Kindness	Bregoli, J. (2008). *The goat lady*. Gardiner, ME: Tilbury House.
	    This is a story of finding the good in people.
	McBrier, P. (2004*). Beatrice's goat*. New York: Aladdin.
	    This book is based on the true account of one family who received aid from Heifer Project International.
	Heifer International (www.heifer.org/)
	    Heifer International is a charitable organization that donates livestock to poor communities around the world.
	Project TEMBO (www.projectembo.org/)
	    TEMBO is a registered Canadian charity that provides funding and support primarily, but not exclusively, to girls and women pursuing educational and small business goals in the Maasai homeland of rural northern Tanzania.

Rising Up and Social Action	Kurusa. (2008). *The streets are free*. Toronto, ON: Annick.
	    This story is based on the experience of children in a low-income neighborhood in Venezuela who fought for the right to turn an empty lot into a playground—a story about organizing to defend your rights.
	Williams, K.L., & Mohammad, K. (2007). *Four feet, two sandals*. Grand Rapids, MI: Eerdmans Books for Young Readers.
	    This book was born when a young girl living in a refugee camp asked the authors of the book who were visiting the camp why there were no books about children like her. I believe this is the most powerful part of the book; the story behind the story. In response the authors crafted a story about 10-year-old Lina, who lives in a refugee camp and is excited to find one sandal in a pile of used clothing brought by some relief workers. Her excitement is momentarily disrupted when she discovers another girl had found the other sandal. In the end the two girls decide to share the sandals. Although the book may not get at critical issues regarding refugees, it does create a much-needed space to raise such issues.
	Youme. (2004). *Selavi, that is life: A Haitian story of hope*. El Paso, TX: Cinco Puntos.
	    This is the true story of Selavi, a street child in Haiti, who shares food and a place to sleep with other street children, and who eventually contributes to opening a home for children and starting Radyo Timoun, Children's Radio, a station run by and for children, which, until March of 2004, was still in operation.
	IndyKids (indykids.net)
	    IndyKids is a free newspaper that aims to inform children about current news and world events from a progressive perspective and to inspire a passion for social justice and learning. According to IndyKids, it is through grassroots organizations and movement-building that people make social change. IndyKids aims to engage young kids in understanding that they can form their own opinions and become part of the larger movement for justice and peace.

REFLECTION QUESTIONS

1. Do you use process drama in your classroom as a way of responding to text? What aspects of drama do you think could be beneficial in your setting? In what ways could they be beneficial? How might you use drama to engage in critical literacy?

2. With your students, brainstorm a list of things that matter, that is, issues or topics that are important to the group. Use the list to reflect on the topics or issues from which you create curriculum. Are the things that matter to your students reflected in your paper curriculum? In what ways might you be able to keep your students' interests at the center of your teaching by negotiating the things that matter to them as curriculum?

3. Think back to a time when you felt your students responded strangely to a text you had read to them or a time when they responded in a way you had not anticipated. What did you do? How did you react? Jot down a few things that you might have done differently if given an opportunity.

CHAPTER 4

Focusing on Social Issues by Bringing the Outside World Into the Classroom

Louis:	In lots of movies, most of the main characters are white.
Kristen:	When you look in a book...no black people.
John:	Yeah.
Kristen:	When you look in a book, it's like, they're white, they're white, there and there and there...and like off in the distance, you find one African American girl.

The school year was nearly over. One late May morning, the children in Lee Heffernan's third-grade public school classroom in a U.S. midwestern town gathered at the rug to discuss *White Wash* (Shange, 1997), a picture book also discussed in the previous chapter. The book was one of several social issues books Lee shared with her students. She defines social issues books as those books that deal specifically with issues such as racism, classism, or gender equity. In this opening exchange, Louis, Kristen, and John use an observation made by Louis regarding a majority of characters being white in movies as a lens through which to talk about books. The exchange is part of one of many conversations that took place as Lee and her students discussed their comments, questions, and connections about such issues as they noticed instances of these outside of school. Lee notes that discussions she has had with her students about books were not like those she has had with them in the past, claiming her students brought up issues that were difficult to understand and sometimes uncomfortable to discuss.

As Lee read *White Wash*, her students eagerly anticipated an opportunity for response. From their previous experience studying picture books with Lee, they knew that the book would be the focus of their reading and writing for several days. They knew this was their teacher's way of bringing issues from their world outside of school into the classroom. Lee used minilessons as a way of teaching specific concepts about a topic, unpacking or analyzing texts such as books, or teaching specific skills.

When she first began reading books that focused on social issues, Lee was surprised by the complex conversations that resulted. Although she was initially hesitant to share such books, the children responded with such enthusiasm that she came to see books as important tools for bringing a critical perspective to their reading and writing workshop. The connections her students were making by focusing on social issues they were bringing into the classroom helped them to become more informed readers and writers.

> Lee: I began by spending several days talking about the books and came to see that lingering with a book over several days had some benefits. First, we were able to talk about a wide range of issues, rather than focusing on one or two main ideas or themes. Second, kids who tended to be quieter found their voice after several days and shared insights that we would have missed. Third, I was able to give myself more time to consider and develop issues from the book that seemed especially significant to all of us.

Lingering With a Book: Six Sessions With a Social Issues Text

Like Lisa Stanzi's second-grade students, whom she describes in her book about creating a literature-based reading curriculum (Galda, Rayburn, & Stanzi, 2000), Lee's students did not come to school knowing how to talk to one another about books. One of the ways she taught them this skill was by giving them sustained time to linger with a book (Short, Harste, & Burke, 1996) while dealing with issues that had importance in their lives. She developed a series of engagements for sharing and studying picture books that she called "six sessions for working with a picture book" (see Table 8). This strategy helped her students to slow down the process of making connections between the book and their lives. She referred to these sessions as minilessons, which she used during readers' or writers' workshop. While discussing the implementation of the six-sessions strategy,

Table 8. Lee's Six Sessions for Working With a Picture Book

Session	Description
Session 1: Read Aloud	Read the book out loud and give students ample time to make connections, comment, and ask questions.
Session 2: Picture Walk	Small groups meet to discuss the book and fill out a response sheet that includes the following prompts: • What is important to remember about this book? • What surprised you about this book? • What questions do you have? • Name a possible writing topic from your own life that relates to the book. The teacher then compiles all the students' questions on one sheet.
Session 3: Small-Group Conversations	Groups of students meet to discuss the question list generated from the response sheets. Then groups monitor their responses to the questions by putting a check mark next to questions that did not generate much conversation and a star next to questions that were discussed at length.
Session 4: Whole-Group Meeting	The class meets as a whole group to discuss the starred questions.
Session 5: Choose an Illustration	The group discusses the illustration from the book that best represents the conversations about it. Once an illustration is selected, it is posted on the learning wall (Vasquez, 1999) along with a caption.
Session 6: Notebook Writing	Each student writes a couple of pages in his or her notebook about the writing topics noted on the response sheet during session 2. These entries are later revisited to determine potential topics to develop further.

Lee commented, "Sometimes I don't go through all six sessions with every book we read together. Sometimes I change the order of the activities or alter them in some way, depending on topics that come up during our conversations."

Lee noted that the number of days it took to go through the various sessions really depended on the book under study and the issues on hand. Here, she details how she used the six-sessions strategy while working with the book *White Wash* (Shange, 1997).

Session 1: Read Aloud

Choose a book that connects with or represents the students' interests or issues from their lives. For instance, Lee chose *White Wash* to read out loud in response to earlier conversations about how much, or how little, power children have in society. She believed the book extended the idea of students taking action with its message of students working together as a group to protect a classmate. Previously, she had shared texts that focused on young people participating in some form of social action. (See Table 9 for an example of a multimedia text set in which characters and people take social action.)

> Lee: As I began reading, the class became focused and quiet. When I got to the scene in the book that described the attack, Quinn interrupted, "You tell us not to write violent stories, so how come you're reading us this book with violence in it?"

Quinn was referring to a previous conversation when Lee and the third graders read a series of books on human rights. She had shared two picture books about slavery along with several other titles. Moved by the slavery texts, half the children had chosen to write slave narratives as they created their own picture book on human rights. Quinn and some other boys had focused on the violence of slavery. Lee suggested to them that their narratives ought to include elements of hope and not to focus solely on violence. Lee responded to Quinn's comment by stating, "This book has more than violence to it. You'll see what I mean at the end."

Session 2: Picture Walk

Session 2 involves revisiting the book for a second time, this time focusing on discussing the storyline of the book as represented by the illustrations. During this session, Lee had the children work with a partner to fill out a response prompt sheet (see Figure 9). She changed the response sheet as needed, but in general it contained the same four to six prompts. For

Table 9. Multimedia Text Set in Which Characters and People Take Social Action

Category	Text Set

Picture Books	Cohn, D., & Rodriguez, L.J. (2005). *¡Si se puede! Yes we can!* Madison, WI: Turtleback.
	   This is a bilingual book about the justice for janitors strike in Los Angeles, California, as told from the perspective of a young boy whose mother becomes a leader of the strike.
	Winter, J. (2008). *Wangari's trees of peace: A true story from Africa.* New York: Harcourt Children's Books.
	   This is a powerful picture book biography that introduces Kenyan environmentalist Wangari Maathai, who won the Nobel Peace Prize in 2004. The story follows the founding of the Green Belt Movement, a movement that advocates for human rights and peaceful democratic change through the protection of the environment.

Websites	The Green Belt Movement (greenbeltmovement.org/gallery.php)
	   This website includes images representing the movement as well as videos and resources.
	Children Helping Children (www.childrenhelpingchildren.net)
	   This is a website with video, photo images, and resources regarding the Children Helping Children organization founded by concert violinist Jourdan Urbach with other child prodigies when he was only 7 years old. The organization is a musical charity foundation that fundraises nationally for pediatric divisions of hospitals and medical charity organizations. Proceeds from Jourdan's Carnegie Hall Debut went to benefit The National Multiple Sclerosis Society.

Music	Don't Close Our School (www.sceps.uklinux.net/selsted.php?l1m=74& m=74) This song is performed by a group of kindergarten to grade six children at Selsted Primary School, located in a small rural community in Southeast Kent in the United Kingdom. Selsted was one of 12 schools earmarked for closure because of falling pupil numbers in the county. In protest, the children and adults of the school formed The Save Selsted Action Group, which then wrote a song to protest its proposed closure.

example, while working with the book *White Wash*, Lee added a new prompt:

> Lee: I added "Why do you think people should or should not read *White Wash*?" to the response sheet for *White Wash* after I thought about Quinn's comments regarding the violence in the book. Prompts are statements or questions that help

Figure 9. Response Prompt Sheet	
Why do you think people should or should not read *White Wash*?	What questions do you have about this story?
What surprised you about this book?	Write one or two writing topics from your own life that connect with this story.
Write one or two statements from someone whose perspective is represented in this book.	Write one or two statements from someone whose perspective is not represented in the book.

the children begin to unpack the book. The kids worked with partners to answer the prompts.

Examples of student responses are included in Figure 10. Lee collated the responses on a single sheet of paper for use in subsequent discussions.

Session 3: Small–Group Conversations

In this session, the collated responses are read out loud, after which time the children are sent off for small-group conversation. Sometimes, however, the read-aloud of the responses is followed by a class discussion.

Figure 10. Some Responses to the *White Wash* Prompt Sheet

Why do you think people should or should not read *White Wash*? • It shows that there are some people that do some really bad things. • You should read it because it teaches you to stick up for others. It has kid power in it!	What questions do you have about this story? • If the girl were white, would the Hawks be mean to her? • Why did she stay in her room for so long?
What surprised you about this book? • That the bad people would paint her face white. • I was surprised that they let go of the brother first. • Everything!	Write one or two writing topics from your own life that connect with this story. • My brother is always mean to me and beats me up. • When I got stitches on my chin, I looked like I had a beard. I had to go to school like that. • Being mad
Write one or two statements from someone whose perspective is represented in this book. • (Helene-Angel) I don't want to go outside! They'll bully me again! • (Helene-Angel) I'm hungry, but I can't eat. I hope I can stand up to them next time. • (Brother) I cannot believe I let those boys push my sister around.	Write one or two statements from someone whose perspective is not represented in the book. • (Brother) Run! Leave her alone! • (Gang member) Man, those stupid kids think they can protect her. Ha! • (Gang member) That shows them! It proves white people are better than black people.

Lee: We read the list of reasons for either reading the book or for censoring the book. Some of the reasons noted by the children for reading *White Wash* were,

- It shows that there are some people that do some really bad things.
- It's a good book.
- It teaches you to stick up for others. It has kid power in it!

As the children reviewed the list, Lee asked them to put a check mark beside any statements that connect in some way to any stories they had written previously. Will immediately shared that both books he wrote in class were about sticking up for other people. Robbie noted that his story in which two teenagers escape from being slaves was about kid power.

Next, Lee and her students used writing to think about inequitable ways of being in the world. At every opportunity, she tried to point out the power in writing about important themes and issues from their lives as one way of uncovering how they may have contributed to maintaining inequitable ways of being and as a way to come up with possibilities for changing inequities in the world.

After a brief discussion about how readers can benefit from reading *White Wash*, Lee asked her students if they thought the book should be censored and why or why not.

Robbie:	I think the book is violent but not too violent.
Will:	Well it's not...I mean it's not like gory and all bloody. They didn't describe it like, "oh look at his bloody arm."
Teacher:	I see. There's a difference?
Will:	It does have some violence but not as much as some other things.
Teacher:	What's something that has a lot of violence, gory violence?
John:	*Scream 2*.
Mark:	*Halloween*.
Tasha:	*Men in Black* has some violence.
Teacher:	So you think the violence in *White Wash* is different than the violence in these movies?

In this exchange, the children make a distinction between exploring violence to discuss consequences associated with violent acts and exploring violence for the sake of repulsing people with blood and gore. Again they use their experience outside of the classroom as a resource for making their point. This discussion about violence in books and movies signified to Lee that her students understood the difference between gratuitous violence and the violence used by authors to depict reality. It also made clear to Lee how easily issues from the children's world outside of school enter into the classroom.

Lee: In retrospect, I wish I had talked more about this issue of violence, focusing more deeply on differences between violence in the newspaper and violence in movies. Also, I could have discussed in greater detail the impact of reading about violence and using violence in our writing. I've come to accept these moments of

20/20 hindsight as part of a critical literacy curriculum. While I work to become more skillful at guiding critical conversations, I also have a greater awareness that conversations are not scripted entities. They have a life and spirit of their own.

After some time, the children were asked to continue their discussion in small groups. Lee had them discuss the list of questions they had about the story from the response sheet. She collated the questions on a sheet of paper and handed out copies to each group. Throughout the year, her students had become very familiar with this process, evaluating questions in terms of how much conversation each generates. The children knew to put a check mark next to questions that did not generate much conversation and a star next to questions that were discussed at length. Lee noticed that this strategy helped her students develop substantive comments for literature circle discussions. During literature circles, small groups of children discuss various topics or issues connected to a particular book they are reading. For example, as Lee's students moved through the list of questions for *White Wash*, one group of three girls and one boy covered a wide range of topics including racism, the issue of the main character's embarrassment over what has happened to her, the motivation of the gang members, and children protecting one another.

Session 4: Whole-Group Meeting

During session 4, the response list is revisited to deal with the issue(s) raised during session 3.

Brad:	She was embarrassed because they put paint all over her face, and she didn't want to go to school. She might have thought that all the kids....
Brenda:	She was afraid.
Kevin:	Like when she walked into school, they'd probably be all laughing.
Teacher:	People might laugh about it?
Kevin:	Yeah.
Lisa:	Well, I think that she might not want to go out because they could have done something a lot worse. They still could do something worse to her.

Will:	Maybe she was just embarrassed because she didn't want to face them [her friends].
John:	Maybe because she let someone paint her face white instead of running away.
Kristen:	Like she might be afraid that her friends would be like, you let a white person attack you like that?
Teacher:	Do you think her friends would do that?
Kristen:	No, but she might think that.
Lisa:	She did say, "I'm an embarrassment to the whole race."
Brad:	And people might say, "You let people paint your face white? And you're trying to be white?" Because I mean, if they didn't know what happened?
Hank:	Maybe if they didn't know how it had happened.
Teacher:	Well, her friends did support her.
Quinn:	At the end.

According to Lee, the issue of shame came up many times in their discussions.

> Lee: It's a difficult issue for me. I tried to focus on the importance of awareness while acknowledging that these topics were emotional and often uncomfortable. There were no easy answers to these questions. While I guided the conversation, I considered myself a participant as we explored issues that troubled all of us. It was clear to me that the kids were ready to talk about the gritty issues in *White Wash*. They were not glossing over the issues in the text but confronting them head on. They were not simply summarizing or merely asking why. They brought in connections from their own lives, the media, other books, and from previous conversations we've had.

Session 5: Choose an Illustration

During session 5, students gather together to choose an illustration from the book to post on the learning wall (Vasquez, 1999, 2005). The learning wall is a large, floor-to-ceiling bulletin board in the classroom that holds important artifacts from the school year—photographs, souvenirs from field trips, newspaper headlines, and more (refer to Table 10 for resources on constructing a learning wall). Each time a social issue picture book is read,

Table 10. Resources for Constructing a Learning Wall

Harste, J., Leland, C., Lewison, M., Ociepka, A., & Vasquez, V. (2000). Supporting critical conversations in classrooms. In K. M. Pierce (Ed.), *Adventuring with books* (pp. 507–512). Urbana, IL: National Council of Teachers of English.

Harste, J., & Vasquez, V. (1998). The work we do: Journal as audit trail. *Language Arts, 75*(4), 266–276.

Vasquez, V. (1999). *Negotiating critical literacies with young children.* Unpublished doctoral dissertation, Indiana University, Bloomington.

Vasquez, V. (2001a). Creating a critical literacy curriculum with young children. *Phi Delta Kappa International Research Bulletin No. 29.* Bloomington, IN: Phi Delta Kappa.

Vasquez, V. (2001b). Negotiating critical literacies in elementary classrooms. In B. Comber & A. Simpson (Eds.), *Critical literacy at elementary sites* (pp. 55–58). Mahwah, NJ: Erlbaum.

Vasquez, V. (2004). *Negotiating critical literacies with young children.* Mahwah, NJ: Erlbaum.

an illustration is selected from the book as a reminder of the conversations about it. A caption is created to go along with each of the illustrations. Both are then posted on the learning wall.

> Lee: The students were familiar with this activity. I told them to think about which picture was most important as I picture walk through the pages of the book. They talked as they decided which illustration to post and defended their choices along the way. With some books, there was clear consensus among the kids. With others, kids chose a variety of illustrations. If no clear choice emerged, I picked a picture that connected with or highlighted our conversations. The conversations about which picture to choose reimmersed us in the text.
>
> For *White Wash* we selected the picture at the end of the book, in which all Helene-Angel's friends come to her house to escort her to school. Together we composed a caption for the picture. One student typed the caption in a large, colorful font and printed it. Another student mounted the picture and caption on construction paper. The page was laminated and stapled to the learning wall (Vasquez, 1999), which by this time of year was filled with striking illustrations from picture books as well as our own classroom artifacts. To me, it looked like a museum gallery or a giant collage. It helped visitors to our classroom know more about our class curriculum and helped us to reflect on our year together.

Session 6: Notebook Writing

In this session, prompt sheets are returned to the students. They are then asked to expand on, in their writer's notebook, the writing topics they identified in session 2. The children are to write at least one page on their topic. When most of them appear to be done, the class is asked to meet. Children who are not finished bring their notebooks with them and continue writing as they listen. The children are asked to take turns sharing their writing. Those who are not ready for sharing have the option of passing, but everyone has to at least share his or her topic with the group. The topics may vary with some being more personal and fun while others are more sociological and serious.

Lee's experience was that children frequently wanted to change their writing topic by this time because newer ideas had come up for them since the first few sessions. For instance, Brad wrote about people making fun of his last name. Will wrote about face painting at the school carnival. Alice, an Asian American student, wrote about being called "Brownie" and "Blacky" by kids at school. Hank wrote about having to take care of his little brother. Meg wrote about her brother having an accident with a can of spray paint in their garage. Brenda wrote about her Sudanese neighbors, "I definitely would not paint their face white!" Kevin wrote about the time he was embarrassed to come to school with stitches in his chin. Blaire wrote about a shooting in the New York subway she had heard about on the news, "Why did someone shoot that person?"

Upon reflecting on session 6, Lee wrote in her journal,

> Our study of *White Wash* came at the end of the school year. Throughout the year, we had used the six-sessions chart with nearly 20 texts. Most of these were picture books, but we also used the chart to study chapter books and a video about social action. I used the six-sessions chart as a tool for allowing more voices to be heard in classroom conversations and for digging deeper into the real-world issues explored in these texts.

In this chapter, Lee made visible the intertextuality of books as she showed how her students drew from their own experiences outside of the classroom and their past experiences with texts to engage in powerful talk. As new issues emerged (violence in writing and media and the trauma of being victimized), the third graders extended their understanding of past topics (racism, shame, and social action). Using social issues texts in combination with other texts was a way to bring real-world issues into the classroom.

In the next chapter, Michael Muise and his fifth and sixth graders also take on real-world issues, attempting to disrupt what they perceive to be unfair school policies. In doing so, they create a space to engage in critical literacy in the math curriculum.

REFLECTION QUESTIONS

1. Reflect on the various kinds of books you share with your students. From those books, what kinds of social issues or topics do the children have opportunities to discuss?

2. Make a list of books or other texts, including multimedia texts such as songs, movies, or websites, through which you could raise social issues. Reflect on your existing curriculum and identify some spaces in which you could use some of these texts to try using Lee's six-session strategy.

3. Record a discussion that you have with your students as you engage with a book. What kinds of questions are raised during these discussions? What do you do with the questions raised? How might Lee's strategy for sustaining conversation change the nature of your conversations?

CHAPTER 5

What If and Why? Critical Literacy, Children's Literature, and Mathematics Investigations

Teacher:	You're not excited about the choices I mentioned this morning? (museum, zoo)
Malcolm:	No. We've done those before. It's the same thing every year.
Teacher:	Hm. I guess I never thought about it that way. Do you have any suggestions about where we might go?
Malcolm:	I just think we should do something fun like a pool party or something.
Teacher:	Well, I'm pretty sure that because of rules the school board has in place that we can't do a pool party. They have concerns about students and safety.
Georgia:	Well, what if we didn't leave and had a day where we had a dance and pizza and then a party here in the room.
Teacher:	OK. That's an idea. Are there any others?
Malcolm:	I think we should go to Canada's Wonderland (amusement theme park).
Class:	Yeah! That's a great idea!

Michael Muise had just begun to explore opportunities for critical literacy with his fifth- and sixth-grade students when the previous conversation took place regarding an end-of-the-year class excursion. Mike's multiage classroom was in an urban elementary school in Toronto, Ontario, Canada. In this chapter you become privy to the ways in which Mike and his students attempted to understand particular school institutional discourse to find the best way to advance their agenda of planning an alternative end-of-the-year celebration. Specifically I share his use of children's literature and math investigations as a way of creating space to encourage the critical reading of social practices in his classroom. Social practices are "particular ways of doing and being, as well as particular ways of acting and talking that are rooted in life experiences" (Vasquez, Egawa, Harste, Thompson, 2004, p. xi). Further, "since different people have different life experiences it follows that social practices are differentially available to various individuals and groups of people" (p. xi). What this means is not everyone has equitable or equal access to literacy or other opportunities.

Imagining What If...

In his journal Mike wrote the following:

> Sarah Perry's (1995) book *If...* entices readers to imagine what if.... What if worms had wheels? What if spiders could read Braille? or What if hummingbirds told secrets? Her book bends the imagination in much the same way a thick piece of glass refracts light, causing one's eyes to see something from a different perspective. I decided to read the book to my fifth and sixth graders. My intent was to use it as a way to generate writing and to inject some creativity and interest in my writing program. I envisioned it to be a way of stretching and pulling at my students' imagination. In the midst of a class discussion about the book, Malcolm asked, "What if we got to pick where we went for our end-of-the-year trip?
>
> I recall trying to reason with my 3-year-old son, Avery, one evening around bath time. I informed him that he had three choices: (1) Get in the tub, (2) Get in bed, or (3) Get your mother. He responded, "But daddy, those aren't my choices. Those are yours." Malcolm, like Avery, was letting me know that my choices were just that—my choices. None of which were my students' choices. Clearly, my ideas for a school excursion were not what Malcolm or his classmates had in mind.

It was early May, and Mike and his students had been talking in class about where they might go for their end-of-the-year outing. He had provided his students with a number of choices including places other classes had visited in the past. The concept of choice, however, was not always clear to him.

Malcolm:	Are all school trips supposed to be no fun?
Teacher:	Well, not exactly, but we do need to let your parents and Mr. Morely [the school principal] know that our trip is tied to what we learned here in class.

Picking up on the what-if theme in the book they had been reading, Mike put forth the question, What if we were to think about our school trip from a mathematics perspective? J.J. responded, "Yeah. We could count the number of people in line-ups, and how much it costs for lunch, and...." It was then that Mike realized how he and his students might be able to use their proposed trip to Canada's Wonderland as a way to show administration and parents how mathematics is used in everyday contexts.

> Mike: Perry's book *If...* led to conversations that helped me to realize the choices I had been providing my students, although well intentioned, were in fact not their choices at all.
>
> Conversation about the book provided a forum for my students to examine everyday school practices such as the policy involved with approving or disapproving school events. In addition, discussion of texts such as *If...* afforded me an opportunity to critically examine my teaching practices.

Mike and his students had predicted that if they could connect the paper curriculum, in particular, the math curriculum that was mandated by the school board, to their proposed school trip to Canada's Wonderland, they would have a better chance of getting their trip approved by the school's administration. To do this, Mike implemented the use of math investigation journals (Schmidt, 1998; Whitin & Whitin, 2004). These were notebooks specifically used to write and think about mathematics-related topics, inquiry questions, and issues. They served as a tool for children to help sort through concepts they know or wish to know regarding mathematics. In their book *Math Is Language Too: Talking and Writing in the Mathematics Classroom*, Whitin and Whitin (2000) describe the use of math journals as a tool for children to talk, write, and reason about topics, issues, and concepts in relation to mathematics. They note that when children do this kind of journaling they are able to move beyond the right answer to engage in a metacognitive exploration of what is going on as they problem solve.

Mike and his students used the journal entries to develop topics for investigation and subsequently to use their discoveries, their new learning, in other situations. The process begins with a student selecting a topic of interest. His students were interested in demonstrating to their parents and the school administrators the academic viability of a trip to Canada's Wonderland. Before beginning their research, Mike had his students map out a plan for their investigation and identify the resources they would be using.

Counting on Frank: Using Math Journals to Produce Data

To get the math investigations started, Mike decided to read to the class *Counting on Frank* (Clement, 1991). In this story, Frank, an inquisitive young boy, finds many uses for his talent of counting. He reveals an uncanny ability to use mathematics to estimate, hypothesize, and theorize about the world around him:

> My dad says, "You have a brain. Use it!" So I do. I sit down and fill my notebook with facts. Did you know that the average ballpoint pen draws a line 7,000 feet long before the ink runs out? My parents consider this fact to be a bit childish, but I'm sure the pen company would like to know. (n.p.)

Mike used the book to set up a discussion for his students to identify math unfolding in the world. Other books that create similar kinds of spaces include *If the World Were a Village: A Book About the World's People* (Smith, 2002) and *One Hen: How One Small Loan Made a Big Difference* (Smith Milway, 2008). *If the World Were a Village* asks readers to imagine the whole world as a village of just 100 people. Using 100 people, Smith addresses a number of different social issues and topics such as illiteracy and languages of power, statistically breaking down how each topic or issue plays out across the globe. Notions of power, control, access, and dominance that come to mind while reading the various statistics create a space for children to develop a different way of reading the world, thereby providing an opportunity for them to understand their own privileges and disadvantages. *One Hen* was inspired by true events. The central character is Kojo, a boy from Ghana, who after the death of his father had to quit school to help his mother collect firewood to sell at the market. With a small loan from the village families, Kojo buys a hen. One year later, he built up a flock of 25 hens. Using his earnings he is able to return to school while maintaining his farm, which grows to become the largest in the region. Included in the book is an exploration of microloans and resources for children to explore. Microloan is a lending system for people in developing countries who have no collateral and no access to conventional banking.

A strategy that would work well using the books previously mentioned, especially in terms of raising awareness regarding the many ways that each of us can contribute to changing inequitable ways of being in the world, is a strategy developed by Whitin and Whitin (2004) that they refer to as *book pairs*. With book pairs, math-related books are used in combination to help children connect math ideas to their everyday world. This is consistent with Short et al.'s (1996) observation that when texts are read in combination, an opportunity is created for children to "extend their understandings of each text differently than if only one text had been read" (p. 537). Each book in the pairing offers students a mathematical lens through which to read the world around them. As part of this strategy, students are given the option of creating their own nonfiction texts based on math-related issues of importance to them while borrowing from the formats of the book pairs they have read.

Mike realized the potential of using books in this way and for taking up other social issues such as gender inequity with books like *Counting on Frank* and the other books previously noted. He also realized how literature could be used as a powerful tool for helping his students name the stories and issues of importance in their own lives. This is in keeping with Christensen's (2000) notion that part of our work as teachers should be to help make visible for our students those things that have been so much a part of their lives that they are taken for granted or ignored. For the time being, however, Mike decided to focus on the Canada's Wonderland project. He asked his students to brainstorm ways in which mathematics was used at Canada's Wonderland. This initiating experience led his students to generate some ideas about where mathematics was used in the daily functioning of the theme park. Each student was then provided with a math investigation journal in which to record thoughts, findings, comments, and questions. (See Figure 11 for examples of the children's work.)

In his journal, Mike wrote,

> I witnessed my students engaged in learning at many levels. Many logged onto the computer searching for websites that could inform their research. Some discovered the role of angles, measurement, time, and velocity in the construction

Figure 11. Examples of Students' Work in Their Math Journals

I learned that in order to build roller coasters builders must use geometry, and measurement to construct the ride. Right angles 90°, 45° and other angles.

(continued)

Figure 11. Examples of Students' Work in Their Math Journals (Continued)

In order for Canada's Wonderland to run as a business they have to take people's money. Money is used so that people can get into the park, buy food and even play games.

(continued)

Figure 11. Examples of Students' Work in Their Math Journals (Continued)

of park rides such as roller coasters. Other students buried themselves in the library, searching out books that explored other theme parks around the world, trying to gather data on such things as park capacities, ride capacities, and group discounts. Others looked at maps of Toronto to identify the quickest and most cost efficient route to Wonderland from our school.

Our classroom engagements around their goal of going to Canada's Wonderland lasted approximately two weeks. As a culminating experience, the students agreed that a letter to the school principal would be appropriate. It was discussed that before we sought permission from parents we should get approval from the school. With this in mind, each student was asked to draft a letter demonstrating what he or she had learned with regard to mathematical uses at an amusement park.

Throughout the following week, the students engaged in formulating a class letter that accompanied their individual letters.

Dear Mr. Morley,

For the past several weeks, Mr. Muise's class has been working very hard to demonstrate to you and the parents that a class trip to Canada's Wonderland would not only be a tremendous amount of fun but also would be a very good educational experience.

In order to support our argument, we decided to explore the many uses of mathematics within the everyday operations of Canada's Wonderland. In our research, which lasted more then two weeks, we discovered that in order for this park to function they have to make use of geometry, currency, time, fractions, division, multiplication, addition, subtraction, probability, velocity, problem solving, and measurement. These are all areas of math that we have looked at this year and in the past.

We feel that we have worked very hard to find several reasons why this trip would be educational. Please consider our trip to Canada's Wonderland. It is something that we all want very badly. We have attached a few of our math investigation journals for you to look at. We hope you will see that we have done a lot of work to show you that this trip would be both educational and safe. We think it would be a lot of fun too.

Sincerely,
Mr. Muise's Grade 5–6 Students

The letter was submitted to the school's principal on a Tuesday afternoon. On Wednesday morning before the children arrived at school, Mike was called into Mr. Morley's office. Mr. Morley wanted to know what the letter was all about. Mike informed him that he had provided the children with the opportunity to choose where they would go for their end-of-year excursion and that the class unanimously decided on a visit to Canada's Wonderland. He reassured the principal that he understood his concerns and shared with him the children's research on the educational value of such a trip.

> Mike: I asked him if he had read the letter and the math investigation journals the kids had completed. He responded that he, in fact, had looked them over and, while he did find them to be most impressive he was unsure how the school board would feel about a group of 10- to 12-year olds going to an amusement park. He informed me that in all likelihood he would have to say no to the class's proposal. I asked him how he planned to let them know that their efforts were fruitless. He asked if I would let them know. I responded by asking him to come to the class and let them know himself. We compromised with a letter from his office.

In his letter to Mike's students, Mr. Morley wrote,

> Dear Mr. Muise's Grade 5–6 Students,
>
> I want to thank you for your letter requesting permission to go to Canada's Wonderland for your end-of-the-school-year trip. It is clear to me that you all have done a tremendous amount of work. I am impressed that you have found so many practical uses for mathematics within the everyday workings of Canada's Wonderland. However, it is unlikely that such a trip would receive school board approval. There are guidelines and regulations that teachers and principals must abide by when considering places to visit for school outings. My main concern arises around the theme park's water rides. There are very strict rules about students participating in any engagements outside of school that involve water. I am sure you will understand that this decision was not an easy one. I appreciate your incredible work efforts.
>
> Sincerely,
> Mr. Morley

It should come as no surprise that Mike's class was disappointed. As he read the letter to them, their shoulders fell and their faces expressed disappointment. Numerous sighs and moans could be heard. Malcolm, however, spoke up and asked, "Who makes the rules for teachers anyway?" Mike told him that many people are involved in creating the rules that are meant to ensure students' time in school is safe and educational. He alluded, however, to the school board as being the primary constructors of such rules. Malcolm then asked who could be contacted at the school board so that he and some others from the class could show how much work had been done in preparation for the proposed trip. Mike told his students that if they wanted to contact someone, the superintendent would be the next logical person. With Malcolm's encouragement, the class decided that a letter should be sent to the superintendent asking for his permission to go to Canada's Wonderland. Over the course of the next few days, the students drafted, edited, revised, and rewrote potential letters to the school superintendent. Following is the letter the children decided to send.

> Dear Mr. Owen,
>
> For the past several weeks, we have been researching the many uses of math within the everyday functioning of Canada's Wonderland. It is our hope that in doing so you will be able to see that such a trip would not only be a tremendous amount of fun, but would also be educational. We sent a letter to Mr. Morley in hope that he would approve our trip, but he said that the rules in place would make it very difficult for him to do so. We are hoping that you can help us in our hope of going to Canada's Wonderland for our end-of-the-year school trip. We have enclosed copies of our math investigation journals in which we did all of our research. You will see that we have found many everyday uses of mathematics at Canada's Wonderland.
>
> Sincerely,
> Mr. Muise's Grade 5–6 Students

Unfortunately, the children never did hear back from the superintendent. They did, however, inquire further with Mr. Morley, who continued to say that without the school board's approval he would not be able to grant permission to go on a trip to Canada's Wonderland.

For the most part, the parents were completely supportive of the children's wishes for their trip. When Mike asked what convinced them such a trip would be a good thing, many of the parents pointed to the math investigation journals as viable data that demonstrated the children had grown academically. Although they were unable to fulfill their hopes of going to Canada's Wonderland, Mike felt it was one of the most exciting experiences for both him and his students.

Using Children's Literature to Create Spaces for Critically Reading Classroom Practice

In spite of the fact that the letter writing and research failed to bring about desired results, Mike was pleased to have had the opportunity for his students to examine the everyday uses of math. In addition, and perhaps more important, they had an opportunity and willingness to act on what they believed. Their initiating experience, born out of Malcolm's response to the book *If...*, provided an opportunity to critically examine existing school practices.

Another strategy for working with texts developed by Whitin and Whitin (2005) is the problem-posing strategy. This strategy connects nicely with the work Mike and his students have done with the book *If...*. Whitin and Whitin explain,

> Problem-posing involves taking a "what-if" stance toward a problem, situation, or story. It consists of describing, modifying and extending the attributes of a story. As children list these attributes, they see a world of related stories embedded within the first story. It has been argued that the more learners change a given story/problem, the better they understand it. (¶ 2)

From Mike's vantage point, discussions that resulted from reading the book provided his students with the what-if metaphor, creating a forum through which his own shortcomings as an educator became visible to him.

> Mike: Before the discussions that followed our reading *If...*, I believed that by providing my students with choices I was able to support my quest for democracy within my classroom. What I was failing to see was how my choices were limiting rather than generative.

Choosing a book that would work in a particular setting is not always easy. Following are a few suggestions to consider when making your choices.

- Choose books that are generative. In other words, choose books that would encourage diverse and varied responses from children.
- Choose books that are aesthetically interesting in their design, color, form, orientation, and language use.
- Choose books that are accessible and meaningful to your students' experiences.
- Choose books that reflect mathematical ideas in interesting and creative ways.

For additional resources and ideas regarding math and children's literature, see the National Education Association's website at www.nea.org/tools/15858.htm.

Finding Ways and Opportunities to Question

Through the exchange of letters, Mike and his students discovered that the decisions about the kind of knowledge that counts in schools are made not only by students and teachers but also by the school administrators. Even though the children in his class had worked diligently researching practical everyday uses of mathematics, convincing school administration that such knowledge is viable and valuable, school board officials ultimately make decisions as to the kind of knowledge that should be valued in classrooms.

Regardless, Mike and his students learned a great deal. His students challenged him to examine how he was attempting to create a democratic classroom and where he was failing to do so. As a community, the students discovered that not everything is distributed equally. Most important, they discovered that power is unequally distributed within the school system. They learned that those in positions outside the classroom value particular kinds of knowledge. They decided, however, that they had ways and opportunities to question all that had been put in place by those outside the classroom. Malcolm had this to say as a result of asking, What if?: "I have learned more from planning this trip than any other even if we didn't get to go!"

As in Mike Muise's fifth- and sixth-grade classroom, in the next chapter, Kevan Miller's first-grade students problematize a particular school-based practice. This time the focus is on creating spaces for critical literacy in the science curriculum.

REFLECTION QUESTIONS

1. Make a list of the last five texts you read to or with your class. For each text, identify what you did. What kind of work did you hope to accomplish? For what area of the curriculum was each text used? What are some ways that you might use books written for children alongside other everyday texts to set up particular discussions in the content areas?

2. Make a list of the various ways that you have used writing in your curriculum. How have you used writing as a response to books? What are some other ways that you might use writing in your classroom as a way for your students to act on issues that matter to them?

3. Reflect on the kinds of choices you make available in your classroom. How might you negotiate choices that take into account issues that are important to your students across the content areas?

CHAPTER 6

What's the Weather? Creating Space for Critical Literacy in the Science Curriculum

What's the weather?

What's the weather?

What's the weather?

What's the weather, everyone?

Is it partly cloudy?

Is it cloudy?

Is there rain?

Or is there sun?

This song was one that all the first-grade children would sing each morning at the school where Kevan Miller taught. Kevan was part of a study group that I worked with from 2001 to 2007 comprised of teachers from Falls Church, Virginia, USA. Our focus was on finding ways to create spaces for critical literacy in the elementary school classroom. Our commitment to the group included keeping journals or noting opportunities through which to construct critical literacies as well as our attempts at working with children from this perspective. Regarding the opening song, Kevan wrote,

> When trying to create spaces for critical literacy throughout the curriculum, I think it's helpful to notice what your students are noticing. I had been singing the weather song with my first graders since I started teaching and I never really thought much about it one way or the other. I was introduced to the song the year I student taught. My mentor and, as far as I knew, all of the other first-grade teachers sang the song with their first graders as part of the daily calendar routine before math and science time. So when I started teaching at the same school,

I sang it, too. Last year was no different, really, except that after the first week of singing the weather song daily, Ronal suddenly looked at me and asked, "Ms. Miller, what about the other weathers?"

While going through the morning routine one day after singing the weather song, Ronal, one of the boys, pointed out that "snowy" wasn't part of the song. At this point the other children began to take notice of what else was missing. "There's no foggy," someone offered. "What about windy?" When Kevan responded, "You're right. What could we do?" several children replied, "Make a new song!" In those few moments, Ronal and the other children were beginning to deconstruct the song and reimagine a new version for themselves that included their understanding of the weather. With this, a class science and math project was born. In this chapter, I spend time in the classroom of Kevan Miller and her first graders as she attempts to frame this newly developed math and science project from a critical literacy perspective.

While reflecting on the progress of this project Kevan noted,

I'd like to say that it was that easy, that after some brief discussion and planning the children started working on a new song that very afternoon. But I had other things planned, and although I don't remember what they were now, I must have thought they were important at the time. Whatever I had planned for the next day must have been important as well. And the day after that. And the day after that.... I loved that Ronal questioned what was left out of the song, and I loved the idea of the children working together to write a new weather song, but in fact almost three weeks passed before I brought up the topic again. The children brought it up a few times at first. Ronal would point out, again, that "snowy" was left out of the song, and several children would ask, "What about our new weather song?" But there were so many other things to do during the math–science block, and as a half-time classroom teacher I was with this class for such a short time already. The weather song was a small part of our few hours together, and there were so many things they needed to learn. When was there time to write a new song?

Starting a Project by Building on Students' Observations

Kevan was certain there wasn't time, but Ronal's observation kept bouncing around in her head. She knew that if this was going to happen, she would have to make the time and create as much space for this work as she could. She began to feel more and more limited by the school-imposed structure of the day and the short time period assigned to the math and science block.

Nevertheless, she decided to not worry about the structure and to raise the question regarding the weather song once again. When she finally mentioned the song to the children one afternoon she was met with some blank looks. Kevan worried that she had missed an opportunity to pursue Ronal's insightful question in what could have been a very interesting project. However, the blank stares quickly disappeared as the children's excitement over the thought of writing a new song returned. Part of their hesitation could have stemmed from Kevan's having put off the discussion in the past. She realized that she had positioned their inquiry question regarding the weather as less important than other aspects of the curriculum. What was most frustrating for Kevan was not being able to carry out her belief of the notion that children learn best when they participate in learning activities that are interesting to them and that have importance in their lives (Comber, 2005; Edelsky, 2000; Vasquez, 2005). In her journal Kevan wrote, "I realized that this was something that was meaningful and important to them. They saw something that needed to be changed, and they wanted to follow through."

Johnston (2004) notes, "Starting with the child's observations rather than the teacher's has many advantages. When children notice things instruction can begin with a joint focus of attention because the children are already attending" (p. 18). This was clearly the case in Kevan's classroom.

As the children carried on with their project they shared what they knew about weather. They started with a brainstorming session and listed the types of weather they felt should be included in the song (see Figure 12). After much discussion they returned to their list and circled the ones they felt were most appropriate based on their experiences. Some of the children also drew images of different kinds of weather (see Figure 13).

The children searched through various books and resources in the classroom library for weather-related books, sorting them and labeling baskets to hold the different categories of weather they had imagined. They read both fiction and nonfiction books—fiction to get a sense of how weather was represented in various texts and nonfiction to gather information on different kinds of weather. They talked about how they might go about rewriting the song.

Figure 12. Brainstorming Chart About the Weather

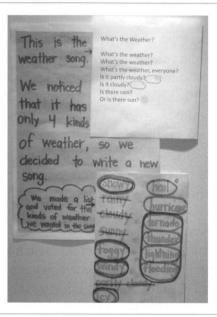

Figure 13. Drawings of the Weather

Tajik: We should keep this song because it has some of the weather.

Gilton: Yeah, we could just add a piece to the bottom.

After more discussion and agreement the students decided to use the original song as a foundation for adding on their new ideas. In doing so they added two new verses. What was interesting about their revised song is the way in which they categorized the types of weather so that one verse dealt primarily with winter weather while the other verse dealt primarily with weather in the spring (see Figure 14). Also interesting to note is that during the students' discussion they decided to include tornado because they had heard of tornado warnings and talked about these in their homes, even though none of them had actually experienced being in a tornado. They also decided to add flooding and thunder and lightning storms because some of them had experienced such weather. When given a chance to bring to the fore their funds of knowledge (Moll, 1992) children are better able to connect more readily with the curriculum. *Funds of knowledge* refers to the accumulated and culturally based knowledge

Figure 14. Redesigned Weather Song

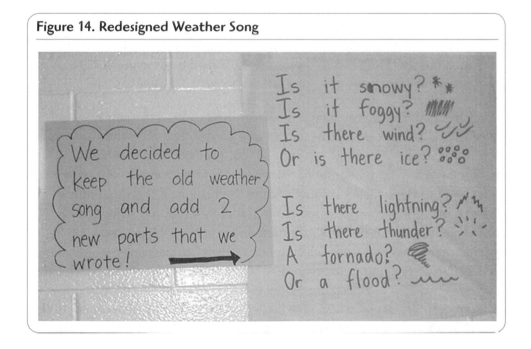

and skills that are part of the children's experiences, which they bring to the classroom. Connecting with the curriculum is what keeps children interested in the work they have before them, often even if that work is complicated or challenging.

The Project Continues

What Kevan didn't realize was that redesigning the weather song was just the beginning. During the time she and her students were working on the song, the children noticed that their weather graph and weather cards, which had been provided in the science kit that all first-grade teachers in the district received, included only certain types of weather as well: sunny, cloudy, rainy, and snowy.

Gilton: Who made the weather graph and cards?

Teacher: They were sent from the county. All first grades use the same things.

Gilton: Do all the first grades sing a song, too?

Kevan reflected,

> With Gilton's remark, our world became a little bit bigger. This wasn't just about our first-grade class anymore. The children realized that the song, the graph, and the weather cards that we used every day were created by someone else, information was missing, and other first grades were (similarly) affected.

Gilton's question moved what had been a very local classroom-based event into a broader arena, the school as a whole, and the school district. Part of the discussion dealt with why all first graders have to sing the same song and who made the decision for this to happen. Being unable to respond to the question brought home the notion of the randomness of some decision-making carried out in the creation and distribution of school curriculum. In Kevan's reflection she considers how the use of specific mandated materials position her students in particular ways. There are assumptions being made regarding what children in first grade should know in the science curriculum, about weather (four kinds of weather), what children are capable of knowing (a limited understanding of weather), and how they should come to this knowing (through the use of the song and chart). She was, therefore, excited to see how the original song-writing project generated other activities and learning.

Having rewritten the song, the children began talking about with whom they ought to share.

Abha: Let's share our song with first grade.

Tajik: No, maybe everybody. Kindergarten, 2nd, 3rd, 4th....

Gilton: Yes, everybody!

Tajik: How can we do that?

Abha: The news!

The children had seen other classes sharing artwork, writing, and skits on the school's daily news program, which was shown on the TV monitors in each of the classrooms. Therefore this was an obvious venue for them and a venue that they felt would give their song some exposure. After some conversation regarding what they should do for the in-school telecast, Kevan and her students videotaped a segment that included Abha, Tajik, and Gilton describing the original, limited version of the weather song followed by a class performance of the redesigned version of the song. It aired on the news later that week.

Redesigning the Weather Graph

Feeling a sense of accomplishment with having rewritten the song, and having performed the song as a demonstration to the rest of the school that things do not have to be as they are, the children moved on to redesign the weather graph. What is interesting about the weather graph is that although it accompanies the song in the weather "kit" the types of weather presented in each is not consistent. The children called attention to this detail as well and kept this in mind as they created their version of the weather graph. Their initial work at trying out the newly revised graph is shown in Figure 15. Here the children basically took a copy of the existing graph and created additional columns and rows to try it out and see how it might look.

Abha created the new chart and included symbols to represent each type of weather listed. Creating the new chart, including deciding on how

Figure 15. A New Weather Graph

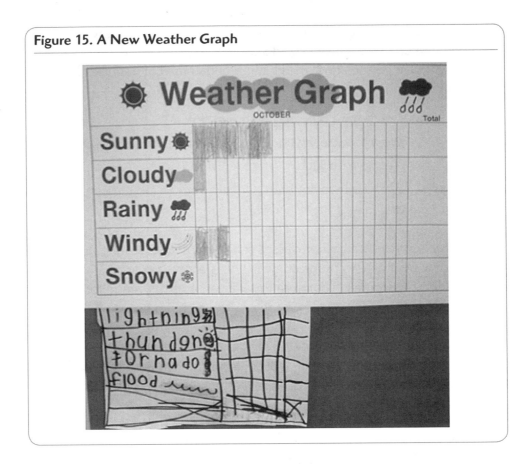

big to make the columns and rows, provided more opportunities for doing science than just filling in squares for a bar graph. The newly created chart is shown in Figure 16.

The children also began writing surveys to try to find out what other first graders knew about weather: "What kind of weather do you like?" and "What is your favorite weather?" They also surveyed the other classes to find out if they might want a new weather graph (see Figure 17).

One afternoon the children worked in pairs and surveyed every first-grade class. They presented their revised weather graph and tallied how many students were interested in having a copy of the graph for their class and how many were not. A few of the children encountered some resistance to the new graph. One boy challenged Gilton and Jose: "But we

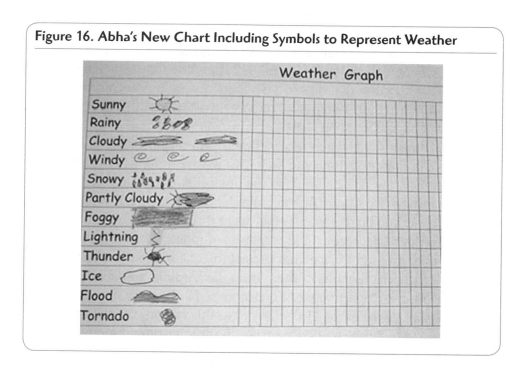

Figure 16. Abha's New Chart Including Symbols to Represent Weather

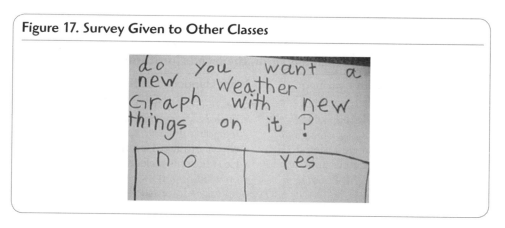

Figure 17. Survey Given to Other Classes

can't have tornadoes here, or floods." When Gilton and Jose shared this with the class, Kevan asked them what they thought about the comment:

Gilton: No! We disagree.

Jose: He can think that. It's OK.

By saying "It's OK," Jose acknowledges that people can have different points of view in spite of Gilton's use of the collective "we" to strengthen his disagreement with the boy. Part of understanding that texts are socially constructed is knowing that different perspectives are represented in texts and as readers whether we agree or disagree matters less than being as informed a reader as possible.

The responses the children received were generally positive, and some classes were curious about making their own weather graph. When it came time to distribute the revised graph to the other first grades, the children decided to include the steps they took to redesign the graph. It was clear that they were energized by the process they went through and wanted to share their discoveries while keeping the possibility of redesign open for others.

In the end, through the weather project the children did not just accomplish the skills required of them from the Virginia Standards of Learning (Virginia Department of Education, n.d.), they surpassed what was required of them. Table 11 demonstrates this notion. On the left side of the chart are two of the standards, one each for science and math. On the right side of the chart are the various skills experienced and learned by the children by participating in the weather project.

Table 11. The Paper Curriculum Versus the Lived Curriculum

Virginia Standards of Learning	What Happened in Kevan's Classroom

Science:
    The student will investigate and understand basic types, change, and patterns of weather. Key concepts include temperature, wind, precipitation, drought, flood, and storms.
Math: Probability and Statistics
    The student will read, construct, and interpret a simple picture and bar graph.
	Science and Math:
	• Explored, researched, and discussed regarding different types of weather and where they occurred
	• Key concepts included a discussion on wind, fog, flooding, snow storms, rainstorms, tornadoes, and hurricanes
	• Surveyed types of weather to be included
	• Read, analyzed, constructed, and designed a weather chart in the form of a bar graph
	• Created and presented new weather song
	• Used technology in creating a video for the school news

Remaining Open to Ideas and Alternatives

Creating space for the children to re-create the weather song sent a message that texts are socially constructed and, therefore, texts can be re-created or redesigned. The notion of texts as socially constructed is one of the key tenets in critical literacy. This in and of itself, however, does not constitute critical literacy. However, it does create space for doing critical literacy work, such as advocating for change and understanding the points of view from which texts are created. For instance, as the children problematized the weather song and chart they did so from the point of view of children who have experienced different kinds of weather. Having experienced different kinds of weather, including flooding for instance, helped them to read the weather song and chart as problematic because these did not represent the experiences of the children for whom they were created.

In a final reflection on this project Kevan wrote,

> There will always be other things to do, plans and obligations that compete for our attention. But what *we* attend to the *children* will attend to, so we need to be open to other ideas and alternatives. We must listen to and acknowledge the conversations in our classrooms, and make time for the opportunities that are presented to us.

In the next chapter, Sarah Vander Zanden picks up on the importance of listening to, acknowledging, and then building from the issues raised by children in her work with her fifth-grade students on unpacking and reimagining a longstanding school practice regarding a nationwide celebration.

REFLECTION QUESTIONS

1. In this chapter, Kevan Miller, the classroom teacher, argues that in order to best support our students, we need to find ways to "notice what they are noticing." Listen closely to the issues your student raise during discussion time or during small-group conversation. Make a list of these issues.

2. Think about one of the issues you noticed your students raising. What resources might you use to further explore this issue? What books and multimedia texts might be useful?

3. Jot down some ideas regarding how you might use the issues raised by children to negotiate a critical literacy curriculum.

CHAPTER 7

Rethinking Arbor Day: Creating Space for Critical Literacy in the Social Studies Curriculum

Eduardo: If they are trying to save trees, then why would they give us pencils?

Siena: What?

Eduardo: Pencils. Duh!

On January 4, 1872, J. Sterling Morton proposed a tree-planting holiday that has come to be known as Arbor Day. Ten years later, in 1882, Arbor Day became a nationwide celebration, which eventually became a ritual celebrated in schools across the United States. Such was the case in spring 2005 when Eduardo and Siena, two of Sarah Vander Zanden's fifth-grade students, were chosen to represent their class at a tree-planting ceremony sponsored by the student council of their school. A few students from each class were invited to a special dedication service, as student representatives, to plant a tree to commemorate Arbor Day. The opening conversation took place as Eduardo and Siena returned to their classroom. The pencils they refer to were those distributed to each participant at the end of the ceremony, as a symbol to remember the day and what it meant.

After overhearing the conversation, in her journal, Sarah wrote,

> I keep thinking about what Eduardo had said. His question was a generative question; it would propel the discussion forward. I knew this because the kids were learning about conservation, and we had read books about this. I expected that they would be able to grasp Eduardo's observations about the contradiction in handing out a wooden pencil to celebrate trees. It was the contradiction, the thought process and observation that mattered.

Sarah had been part of a critical literacy study group. This is in fact the same study group to which Carol Felderman, whom you will meet in Chapter 8, and Kevan Miller whom you met in Chapter 6, belonged. As part of her work with the critical literacy study group, Sarah kept a journal of literacy moments and events that unfolded in her classroom. Reflective writing was a tool Sarah used to rethink her teaching practice as a way of better supporting her students' needs. In her journal she wrote about and reflected on larger issues her students were raising, as well as intersections between the real curriculum in her classroom and the mandated curriculum of the state of Virginia. The pencil incident is a good example of this point of intersection, whereby the mandated social studies curriculum that resulted in the Arbor Day celebration resulted in the underlying issue of conservation raised by Eduardo when he asked, "If they are trying to save trees, then why would they give us pencils?"

This point of intersection is further illuminated in the following journal entry.

> Sarah: Eduardo had noticed a contradiction and was raising questions about this observation in a respectful way. He was a "special" participant, one of a select few who could attend this dedication. We had read a lot about conservation in the weeks building up to this event and discussed them as a class. We had studied erosion, weathering, and human impact on the Chesapeake watershed through fieldtrips, in class experiments, and research in the first quarter of the school year. I included some texts that would reinforce key curricular ideas surrounding Landforms and Human impact on the land, as specified in the Fairfax County POS (Program of Study) and Virginia Standards of Learning (SOLs) because it was now the third quarter and the year end high stakes tests were coming.

Even though Sarah fully believed in, and was very good at, building social studies curriculum from the interests of her students, she was very cognizant of what children were expected to know to be successful at the high-stakes tests that they would have to take. Knowing the demands of the mandated curriculum made it easier for Sarah to engage in teaching practices she felt would be most supportive of her students' inquiry questions and interests because she was able to identify where the mandated content was addressed in this nonmandated work.

Setting a Context for Social Issues in the Social Studies Classroom

During one of our study group meetings, Sarah shared her experiences in working with her students to focus on class discussion as a means to articulate their opinions and advocate for their needs and as a way of promoting access to the school curriculum for her fifth-grade students who might struggle in academic settings. The class was her first "official" experience with an inclusion classroom. She had always had seven or so students with learning differences in her class, but she had never had as many English-language learners at varying levels of second language acquisition, and more than 60% of the class on free or reduced-cost lunch because their family's income fell below the poverty line. This year's class was definitely one of the most linguistically and culturally diverse groups of children with whom she had ever worked.

In a journal entry she shared with the group she wrote,

> Although all of the classes at the school had many speakers of other languages, the range of languages and experiences in this group was the most diverse I had worked with yet. Students and their families' came from 12 countries (Pakistan, Guatemala, Mexico, El Salvador, Cuba, Nicaragua, Costa Rica, Philippines, Cambodia, Laos, Nigeria, and the United States) and spoke at least 12 different languages before English. Two of the 21 were English speakers first. Most students spoke at least two languages, their home language and English, with varying ranges of English proficiency. Three of the students were bilingual in Spanish and English and participated in the Spanish Immersion class. Another way the class was diverse aside from linguistic diversity was that this class was also a designated inclusion class. This meant many students with specific learning needs (half of the group) were intentionally placed in our cotaught classroom. One student had full-time assistance due to significant physical needs, while others students benefited from extra support during the cotaught language arts block. Though many students had academic needs, there were also many who excelled academically, for example five students were involved in the county gifted and talented program.
>
> Students' life experiences also varied greatly. When I asked the class to share stories of how they came to the school as a way to get to know each other, stories including tracing how their families came to the United States. This year stories included describing the Killing Fields in Cambodia, political persecution in Nicaragua and El Salvador, tracing the history of a former slave family from South Carolina, a father pursuing a graduate degree in the U.S., as well as moving from another part of the county or from another state. Many shared their families' general hopes for a better education for their children. Not all of the stories

students shared were extreme, but they were different and illustrated for me the unique makeup of the class.

While keeping her students in mind, in another journal entry Sarah wrote,

> My goal [this year] was for all of the students to be active participants in class, so we spent a great deal of time cultivating a classroom community devoted to listening to one another and learning how to accept that different kids have different needs and that was OK. I explicitly taught kids how to disagree in the classroom and on the playground, as well as how to notice what others were doing so that we could be more respectful of our classmates and be better peer supports in academic settings.

Sarah and her students also engaged in many civics-oriented projects such as collecting materials needed by an animal shelter and exploring environmental conservation. As part of this work Sarah read literature that helped her students think differently about certain topics or issues or that provided different ways of thinking about an issue or topic. She believed offering her students ways of looking at things from multiple perspectives was an important life skill. She often used books, both fiction and nonfiction, to provide such perspectives and as a jumping off point for discussion. As a group, Sarah and her students read books like *Stand Tall, Molly Lou Melon* (Lovell & Catrow, 2002), which deals with issues of difference; *Seed Folks* (Fleischman, 2004), which focuses on participation in community; and *The Wump World* (Peet, 1991) where aliens use up Earth's resources. This last book, in particular, sparked lots of discussion about the impact our everyday actions have on the world around us, and heightened the group's awareness of observing the world from an environmentalist perspective. Consequently, Sarah's students were not naïve when it came to taking on projects focused on social issues. This is the background experience that framed Eduardo's question regarding the Arbor Day pencil.

Plant a Tree and Make the World a Better Place

In one of her journal entries, Sarah talks about the generativeness of Eduardo's question especially given the experience the children had previously with issues regarding the environment and conservation. She notes that Eduardo making problematic the contradiction in handing out pencils at an Arbor Day celebration is what would make the difference. She was right. His question resulted in sustained conversation about the issue.

Sarah wondered what her other students thought about the Arbor Day incident and hoped that Eduardo's comment would generate topics for study. Conversation during class meeting had been a successful venue for the majority of her students to participate throughout the year and she wanted to take the opportunity to explore how much some of the children had grown in this respect. The comment came from Eduardo, a student who had been less engaged in the class since the beginning of the year. Despite how hard Sarah tried to keep the curriculum accessible to him, there were many times when he found it difficult to participate and seemed disinterested in the topics being studied. Nevertheless, Sarah continued to work with him on repositioning himself in the classroom, by doing things like identifying people with whom he might want to work or creating space for him to join in classroom conversations by helping him articulate his ideas. She had hoped to make learning more accessible and interesting for him. She tried to help him find classmates with whom he shared common interests and tried to draw out of him what topics and issues he was interested in pursuing.

Sarah brought the children together for discussion. While the group sat around a circle, she started the conversation by restating what Eduardo had said the day before. Her students were used to discussion and had often sat in the circle for class meeting, book discussions, and content lessons. Early on in the year she had spent time with them on what it means to have respectful conversations. She talked with her students about the importance of turn taking during discussion time. She also talked with them about it being acceptable to disagree with one another as long as during the conversation, each student who had something to say was given an opportunity to do so. She shared with them that class meeting time was as an opportunity to talk with others in the class about their burning issues, such as the Arbor Day incident. This process was, therefore, familiar to them.

Teacher: What do you think about what Eduardo said?

Immediately the fifth graders jumped into the conversation:

Ansony:	So what if they give you a pencil? I didn't get one.
Sanya:	They could have given you a paper to share at home, I would share it.
Milton:	Maybe they thought that if they gave papers, kids would throw them and they won't throw pencils.

Ansony's comment and the responses by Sanya and Milton are representative of the normalized or naturalized treatment of Arbor Day in many school settings where students participate in set rituals as passive observers. It is easy to see how this normalization comes into being when looking more closely at resources available to teachers regarding celebrating this day. For instance phrases like "Celebrate Arbor Day and take positive action" or "Celebrate Arbor Day to make the world a better place" represent the sorts of sentiments that pepper resource documents on Arbor Day. In an Internet search on "Studying Arbor Day" or "Unit of Study on Arbor Day," for instance, I found resources like the Arbor Day Alphabetic Order Worksheet from www.teachnology.com and a cloze activity called Clozing the Deal on Arbor Day from www.teachers.net, whereby students are asked to identify 12 words having to do with Arbor Day, learn to recite and use these words, and then use the words in context by means of a class sentence bee.

Neglected are opportunities to historicize and unpack the day as one with political roots whereby people who moved into the Nebraska Territory in the 1800s proposed the holiday at a meeting of the State Board of Agriculture and where eventually what has come to be known as Arbor Day came into being as a result of an official proclamation. Lost are opportunities to explore reasons beyond "greening" as the impetus for such a day. For instance, Heger (2000) notes that J. Sterling Morton, who founded Arbor Day in 1872, was an ardent opponent of the tariff protecting the U.S. lumber industry from foreign competition and that he had another motive behind his Arbor Day advocacy. According to Heger,

> [Morton] detested the protective tariff that enriched the U.S. lumber industry and depleted native forests. He wanted to break the power of the tariff. So his secondary Arbor Day message was: Plant a tree and strike a blow for free trade (¶ 3).

This is a far cry from the passive save-the-world-through-celebration rhetoric in "Celebrate Arbor Day and make the world a better place."

Redesigning Existing Practice

As the conversation continued, the students began to come up with alternate solutions, in a "redesign" of what artifact, other than a pencil, could have been handed out at the event. This sustained conversation, of which a portion is included below, resulted from the children's desire to get the message out regarding ways of respecting the environment, to more than just the special group who was allowed to attend the Arbor Day event.

Eduardo: We need to save trees, save the environment, not cut down trees. They are lying.

Teacher: Who is "they"?

Reston: Professionals who protect trees. Probably.

Siena: The PTA.

Teacher: Why?

Siena: They got the tree.

Eduardo: The government.

As the children continued to unpack the context in which the event took place, they began a conversation about the larger systems in place and how things are decided. Gee (2004) refers to these social ways of being as systems of meaning. He describes these systems as comprised of complex interactions and relationships that shape the way things are. These are held in place by Discourses, a community's ways of doing, being, thinking, acting, and so forth. The children recognize that things don't just happen; there are decision makers out there and there is nothing natural or neutral about the process of deciding the way the day is celebrated and what memento might be appropriate to represent the day. This lends itself to the development of a worldview that is more active than reactive. If you can identify the decision makers—those in power—you can then think in a different way about the decisions being made, generate new ideas, and contribute to disrupting the problematic practice and contribute to change.

Mei-an: Yeah, maybe they have so much extra wood that they made pencils for the kids.

Siena: Yeah, it could be recycled wood. (Examines pencil)

Eddy:	Well, where do they [pencils] come from? Why not use plastic instead of wood?
Claro:	Well, when they cut down the trees, they have to plant another one. So maybe they did that. But they could just make a commercial and not cut down any trees and everyone would see it, not just Cheto and Siena. I mean, fliers and pencils both use wood and we don't even know what they wanted now...because we weren't there.

As the group considers alternate perspectives, Claro noticed his classmates struggling with the issue of "the Arbor Day pencil." In response, he begins directly teaching about tree conservation when he says, "Well, when they cut down trees, they have to plant another one...." He also talks about how to make this kind of information accessible to a wider audience stating, "they could just make a commercial...and everyone would see it...." He also raises the issue of not knowing the position from which the Arbor Day event was planned saying, "we don't even know what they wanted... because we weren't there." In other words, Claro makes the point that they do not really know the intent of the event planners in handing out the pencil or why they chose such an artifact to commemorate the day. He knows there is an underlying message that comes with the event but what that is exactly is unclear. Nevertheless, acknowledging that someone wanted to get some message across demonstrates Claro's knowledge that texts, including the event as a "text" to be read, are socially constructed and that they are constructed from particular perspectives, beliefs, and ideologies. This goes along with Sarah's belief of the notion that the world, events, places, things, print matter, and so forth, can all be read, interpreted, and analyzed in some way.

The conversation continues as follows:

Christian:	I disagree, factories have to make pencils, and they use energy so they might cut down more and just use the extra wood to do the pencils.
Reston:	I disagree with Eddy, because we can't sharpen plastic pencils. Mechanical would be better.
Marisol:	You can sharpen plastic pencils.
Michael:	Yeah, lead is better, mechanical.

Reston: Wait, I disagree with Michael now, even though they wouldn't use wood, they are using other resources. Which resource is better? It's like *The Wump World* [Peet, 1991]. Wait—how do you get lead?

In this exchange, the students begin to stray from the underlying social issue as they discuss whether plastic or mechanical pencils would be better. Eventually they return to *The Wump World*, highlighting the human impact on the environment and making connections to information previously learned through class work about resources and energy. Since the beginning of the school year, the children had gotten better at using one text (e.g., *The Wump World*) to read another text (Arbor Day as a social text). They have learned that to better critically analyze a situation, one needs to frame it using a different discursive perspective. *The Wump World* created a space for them to do this. Framing their understanding of the Arbor Day event from the lens of *The Wump World* helped the children to better articulate their thinking.

Kazin: For real, if they gave mechanical pencils they would waste more money for them. It's just a dumb reminder; they wouldn't waste that much money on us.

Kazin's comments were made out of frustration over the distribution of the pencil and the conversations with his classmates. He had felt that some of his classmates should have been more concerned about the underlying issues or conservation. His comments during the class meetings on this topic focused on different possible realities. Were pencils distributed as an inexpensive and unnecessary token? Was this inexpensive token reflective of the organizers attitude, specifically that "pencils were good enough for the children"? When Kazin says, "they wouldn't waste that much money on us," he is referring to any memento that might cost more than a pencil, such as a mechanical pencil. Either way certain that little thought was given to the event as a whole, thus his reference to the pencils as "dumb reminders."

The idea of reminders is an interesting one when set in the context of schools as rule governing institutions. Was the pencil meant to be a reminder of the moral lessons associated with the event, whatever those may have been? If so, Kazin seemed almost insulted that such a reminder was felt by the organizers to be necessary.

Gabriela: Who decided it anyways? Maybe we should write a letter.

To get responses to some unanswered questions regarding the decision-making process around Arbor Day, and as a form of social action, Gabriela suggests writing a letter. She made this recommendation based on her past experiences and success in getting issues resolved through letter writing. For instance, in the past she had written a letter to be included in the yearly special education conference her parents attended at her school regarding how to best support her learning. Eduardo, Siena, and Kazin, who first noticed the ridiculousness of distributing pencils on Arbor Day, took up Gabriela's suggestion and wrote a letter to the Parent–Teacher Association. Further, they submitted comments on a couple of websites focused on Arbor Day. Siena also met with the student council association president and staff representative about making the Arbor Day ceremony accessible to all students instead of limiting the event to a chosen few.

The Arbor Day incident took place at the end of the school year when the fifth graders were about to leave the school to attend a middle school nearby. Sarah, the classroom teacher, also left the school to pursue doctoral studies. Unfortunately, as a result, there was no follow up on what resulted from the letter writing and meeting with the student council president and staff representative. After the fact, Sarah did hear that the staff representative, who eventually took on the role of assistant principal at another school, disagreed with the students' concerns and found nothing problematic about privileging some students by inviting them to attend the Arbor Day event while marginalizing others when they are flatly denied an opportunity to do so.

Critical Literacy as Changing Participation

Barton and Hamilton (1998) note,

> Literacy is primarily something people do; it is an activity, located in the space between thought and text. Literacy does not reside in people's heads as a set of skills to be learned, and it does not just reside on paper captured as texts to be

analyzed. Like all human activity, literacy is essentially social, and it is located in the interaction between people. (p. 3)

The interactions engaged in by Sarah's students provided for them space to imagine how existing social practices could be otherwise. This work not only addresses the school district's standards of learning (5.7f), but surpasses the identified key concept: human impact (on the environment). Within the context of attempting to disrupt problematic Arbor Day practices at their school, they began to consider how what they had come to know and believe is shaped by "specific participants in a literacy event and the context itself" (Larson & Marsh, 2005, p. 11). In their letter writing and subsequent meetings with the student council representatives, they began to interrogate the decisions made by these participants as well as the notions associated with the normalized Arbor Day celebration. At the same time, they were gaining experience in reimagining a problematic school practice, which helped them to consider ways they could participate differently in the world of school and beyond. As suggested by Janks and Comber (2005), involving young people in the process of text production, editing, and design demonstrates to them that texts are not neutral or natural. This work also helps young people to understand that language is a powerful tool for doing different sorts of life work and that how we constitute things and how we are constituted through social practice makes a difference in the ways we are positioned in life and the positions from which we are able to speak or participate in the world.

Larson and Marsh (2005) note that people learn by participating in culturally valid activities. Even though the letter writing and the meetings may not have been successful in accomplishing the work the children had imagined, the experience provided a space for them to participate differently in school as active players rather than passive recipients of school and everyday texts.

In the next chapter, we spend time with Carol Felderman's second-grade students as they explore the use of podcasting as a tool for participating differently within their classrooms and beyond.

REFLECTION QUESTIONS

1. Think about the various events held at your setting along with traditions that have been passed on over the years at your institution. Reflect on

how these events and traditions were started, by whom, and for what purposes. Whose interests are served by holding such events? Are there those for whom such events are not accessible?

2. In light of the Arbor Day pencil incident, reflect on the language used to describe such events as well as the symbols used to represent these events.

3. How might you use social texts such as school events and traditions from which to build a critical social studies curriculum?

CHAPTER 8

A Podcast Is Born: Critical Literacy and New Technologies

Scarlett: Hi! My name is Scarlett. You might remember me from the musical last week. This week we will tell you about how we're going to save money for the trip to the Baltimore Aquarium in Baltimore, Maryland, USA. We will tell the story of how we are doing this. [¡Hola! Me llamo Scarlett. Puede ser que me recuerdas de la parte musical de la semana pasada. Esta semana les vamos a contar sobre como vamos a ahorrar dinero para el excursión al Acuario de Baltimore en Baltimore, Maryland, USA. Vamos a contarle el cuento de cómo vamos hacer esto.]

Ben: Hi! My name is Ben and this is how it began. Our class had a meeting about the trips of the year. Scarlett was the one that asked if we were going to go to the Baltimore Aquarium this year. Ms. Maggie, our teacher, told us we could not go because it costs too much money. We didn't agree with our teacher. Then I said we could sell things to save money for the trip. [¡Hola! ¡Mi nombre es Ben y esto es como empezó! Nuestra clase tuvo una reunión sobre las excursiones del año. Scarlett fue la que preguntó si íbamos a ir al Acuario de Baltimore este año. Nuestra maestra Sra. Maggie nos dijo que no podíamos ir porque cuesta demasiado dinero. Nosotros no estuvimos de acuerdo con nuestra maestra. Entonces yo dije que podíamos vender cosas para ahorrar el dinero para la excursión.]

Scarlett: We decided to have a meeting with [the principal]. We sent him a letter via e-mail and took a copy to his office. He gave us an appointment for Friday. We believe that the meeting was good. Then we started to prepare all the hard work. We cannot wait to see what will happen tomorrow. [Decidimos de tener una reunión con (el director de la escuela). Le mandamos una carta por correo electrónico y llevamos una copia a su oficina. El nos dio una cita para el viernes. Pensamos que la reunión era buena. Entonces empezamos a preparar todo el trabajo duro que íbamos hacer todo este año. Otra vez hicimos carteles y enseñamos a nuestros compañeros como hacerlos. Esta vez más clases participaron. No podemos esperar para ver lo que va a pasar mañana.]

The opening exchange represents how the children in Carol Felderman's second-grade classroom used podcasting as a tool for conveying messages about projects they were doing or for sharing their thinking on topics or issues that were important to them, both locally, such as advocating for certain privileges, and globally, such as global warming or environmental issues. A podcast is an on-demand Internet broadcast or show that is either in audio or video format. On demand refers to the portability of the show whereby listeners could either listen or watch using their desktop or laptop computer or upload the show onto their digital player or other mp3 listening device that organizes and plays audio or video files. Listeners can also subscribe to a podcast so that they can receive new shows as they are released.

Carol and her second graders took on the role of podcaster during the spring of 2007. A podcaster, the person(s) doing the podcast, records either audio or video of themselves or others, using a digital recorder (see Figure 18) and then uploads it, or posts it to a place on the Internet for others to hear or view. Most modern laptops have built-in sound cards, which allow you to use inexpensive microphones to record directly into the computer using software such as Audacity (www.audacity.sourceforge .net) or Garageband (www.apple.com/ilife/garageband/). The quality of the recording is not as good but is also dependent on the quality of the microphone. Another option is to use a recording device that uses a USB interface to the computer. Recordings are done directly into the computer using software as noted previously. The quality of the recordings is remarkably better than using the built-in sound cards. (Refer to Table 12 for steps to subscribe to a podcast and Table 13 for a list of recommended

Figure 18. Digital Recording Devices

Table 12. Subscribing to a Podcast

Steps	Procedure
Step 1	Install a podcatcher (podcast receiver where you can download podcasts for listening and/or viewing). There are several choices that are available for free. Two of the most popular are iTunes and Juice. Both of these can be used with Windows (PC) or Macintosh (Apple) units. Free Podcatchers • itunes: www.apple.com/itunes/ • jpodder: sourceforge.net/projects/jpodder • juice: juicereceiver.sourceforge.net/ • myPodder: www.podcastready.com/ Or you could go to the Podcatcher Matrix site (www.podcatchermatrix.org/) where you can compare a number of different systems to decide on which one best suits your needs.
Step 2	Once you have installed a podcatcher, copy the link from the RSS feed of the show (RSS is a format for delivering web content that changes regularly as in podcasts that release new shows on an ongoing basis). This is usually an orange button marked XML or RSS.
Step 3	Paste the link into your podcatching client. Once you have completed steps 1–3, new shows on podcasts to which you have subscribed will download automatically whenever you ask your podcatcher to update your files. There is no limit to the number of podcasts to which you can subscribe.

Table 13. Recommended Recording Devices

Name	Manufacturer	Approximate Cost
EDIROL R-09HR	www.edirol.net	$350
Olympus DS-40	www.olympusamerica.com	$100
Sony ICD-SX700	www.sony.com	$150
Zoom H2	www.zoom.com/	$150
Zoom H4	www.zoom.com/	$200
Zoom H4n	www.zoom.com/	$350

recording devices.) In their show, the second graders often included Spanish because a good number of the children in the school were native Spanish speakers learning English, and many of those who were native English speakers were in the Spanish Immersion program. The dual-language episodes made the messages being conveyed by the children more accessible to Spanish speaking members of the school community and their families.

The sign in Figure 19, which was prominently displayed in Carol Felderman's second-grade classroom, attests to how the children felt about taking on podcasting as a new communicative practice, or way of communicating events, thoughts, and ideas.

Figure 19. Podcast Sign

Comber, Nixon, and Reid (2007) note that in the teaching of literacy, our role as teachers includes extending the repertoires of literacy and communications practices available to our students. They claim what we need is a pedagogy of responsibility, which is about "classroom practice that is informed and structured by teachers' commitment to engaging with questions of diversity and democracy" (p. 14) with their students. Place-based pedagogies, they say, foreground the local and the known and are opportunities for teachers "to structure learning and communication experiences around the things that are most meaningful to their students: their own places, people and popular cultures, and concerns" (p. 14). They ask how technology, such as sending a message or text using a cell phone, creating a video, or participating in online spaces such as electronic art galleries for children, provide new and interesting ways for children to communicate their ideas, questions, and understanding about the world around them. Comber and her colleagues further note,

> Literacy teaching cannot, and we believe it should not, be a content-free zone. We know that there is great potential for students to expand their literate repertoires when they become deeply engaged in acquiring new knowledge about things that matter.... (p.14)

There is a line in the movie *Cars* (Lasseter & Ranft, 2006) where Sally, one of the main characters, reflects on a time when roads and roadways moved with the land rather than cutting through it. She specifically was referring to the famous Route 66. She lamented that back then, "Cars didn't drive on the road to make great time; they drove on the road to have a great time." In pedagogies of responsibility and place as described by Comber and her colleagues (2007), the journey matters. This chapter focuses on a journey into the world of podcasting by a group of second graders and the transformative effects that resulted from the experience. As part of this, I will explore the ways in which this new technological tool intersects with critical literacy.

New Technologies as Tools for Engaging in Critical Literacy Work

In Chapter 1, I included a set of tenets through which I engage with critical literacies in the classroom. These are the same tenets I attempt to share with other teachers in my conversations with them regarding creating spaces for critical literacy in their settings. The last tenet, which states that text design and production can provide opportunities for critique and transformation, is really where new technologies and social media could have a strong role. Text design and production refers to the creation or construction of texts and the decisions that are part of that process. This includes the notion that it is not good enough to simply create texts for the sake of "practicing a skill." If children are to create texts they ought to be able to let those texts do the work intended. For instance, if children are doing surveys or petitions they ought to be done with real-life intent for the purpose of dealing with a real issue. If children write petitions they ought to be able to send them to the person for whom they were intended. Helping children understand real-life functions of text is an important component of growing as a literate individual.

Lankshear and Knobel (2007) ask the question, What can new technologies afford literacy work in schools? In this chapter I am particularly concerned with the question, What can new technologies and social media afford our work with critical literacy? Social media tools such as podcasting and blogging allow people to connect electronically using the Internet. *Social media* refers to the integration of technology and social interaction online.

This question, of what new technologies afford the work we do, rings especially true in the area of text design (creating written, drawn, or electronic texts), or redesign (taking existing texts, critiquing their construction and then creating new texts), and production (producing or constructing texts). I want to be clear that the use of new technologies and social media does not constitute engagement with critical literacies. Just because one is using new technology in the classroom does not mean they are simultaneously engaging in critical literacies. Rather these new technologies and social media can be used as tools within our critical literacy work. Such tools can be used in the production of texts and also in the distribution of texts both locally and globally.

The potential impact of using new technologies to make accessible to others the work we do is astounding. For instance, researchers at The Diffusion Group, a consumer technology research and marketing firm, recently predicted that the U.S. podcast audience will climb from 840,000 in 2005 to 56 million by 2010 (The Diffusion Group, 2005). And what started out as a system for distributing homespun radio programming over the Internet has now caught on with big media companies such as ABC News, NBC News, ESPN Disney, and National Public Radio, who have all introduced podcast programming in recent months. Libsyn is a popular podcast host site. Lee (2006) of The Marketing Loop notes that according to the Libsyn data, more than 45 million people listened to and watched podcasts off the Libsyn network alone in the first quarter of 2006. comScore Inc., a global Internet information provider that maintains databases regarding ways in which the Internet is used and the wide variety of activities that are occurring online, reported that in December 2008, the Internet surpassed one billion global users (Gavin, 2009). This statistic refers only to individual users and does not include those who use Internet cafés or computers in public settings such as libraries. Given these statistics it's not so much of a surprise that the Oxford University Press (2005) selected *podcast* as Word of Year in 2005. It competed against words like *trans fat* and *bird flu* (www.us.oup.com/us/brochure/NOAD_podcast/).

Also, given the proliferation of computer access around the globe, it is important to consider the question of whether children of the 21st century are disadvantaged when they are not given opportunities to grow at least some understanding of the ways in which new technologies can be used to do particular kinds of work in our everyday lives. This is particularly important in places where hardware and software is readily available. The shame of the matter is that access to the hardware and software is not the primary problem. The major issues lie in the lack of training for using technology and in particular opportunities for teachers to imagine the role technology could play in their curriculum, not as an add on but as an integral part.

New Technical Stuff and New Ethos Stuff

What new things can we do, in terms of literacy teaching and learning, with the use of technology, and what can we do differently in our teaching as a result? In terms of thinking about possible affordances, a differentiation between Web1.0 and Web2.0 is useful (see Table 14 for examples of Web1.0 and Web2.0 software). In the Web1.0 world, information flows in one direction. Webpages, for instance, are static and only allow the viewing or reading of content on the page. Blogs, on the other hand, in a Web2.0

Table 14. Examples of Web1.0 and Web2.0 Software

Examples of Use	Web1.0 One-way flow of information	Web2.0 Interactive software that allows a user to participate in open sharing of content through various social networking tools on the Internet.
Photographs	Kodak Gallery (Ofoto) www.kodakgallery.com	Flickr www.flickr.com/
Reference	Britannica Online www.britannica.com	Wikipedia www.wikipedia.com
Content organization	Personal webpage	Blog

world allow users to participate in open sharing of content through various social networking tools on the Internet. Networking tools like Flickr (www .flickr.com) allow users to not only share photos but also organize, link to other Flickr users' photos, comment on one's own and others' photos, and assign various levels of copyright to photos so that they can be used by other web users. Photos can also be tagged, meaning they can be categorized, so that they are "discoverable" (formerly referred to as *searchable*) on the Internet. Readers also are encouraged to comment on blog posts and share links to other related sites. What this does is create a stronger presence for the blogger or user of social networking tools. A strong presence draws more traffic to a blog site, making information being shared much more accessible and widespread. In their differentiation, Lankshear and Knobel (2007) use the terms *new technical stuff* and *new ethos stuff*. New technical stuff refers to living in a digital culture, or digitality, and what that affords: connectivity, social networking, and instant information. The new ethos stuff refers to a shift of mindset, or way of thinking about technology use, as a result of the new technical stuff.

In terms of podcasting, the focus of this chapter, the question here is, What does podcasting afford the work done by the second graders? Said differently, what sorts of possibilities for connecting with the world outside the classroom are made available through the use of this social networking tool and specifically, how might this tool be used in carrying out their critical literacy work?

Podcasting With Second Graders: Getting Started

Carol Felderman's second-grade students were born into a world that is technologically very different from the world she and I were born into. The statistics I shared earlier regarding the number of Internet users today attests to this. It was not surprising, therefore, that many of the children came to school with knowledge of and experience with the new technological stuff and new ethos stuff described by Lankshear and Knobel (2007). Their interest in podcasting was, therefore, not a surprise.

The second-grade classroom is located in a school with more than 800 students. According to the school website, the students represent more than 40 countries of origin and more than 20 different languages spoken at home, although the dominant of these is Spanish. The neighborhood is located about 25 minutes outside of Washington DC, in a neighborhood that is experiencing increased gang activity and where most of the children receive free or reduced-cost lunch. On average there were 20 students in the class. Fifty percent of the children were English-language learners. Sixty-five percent received free or subsidized meals. There was one student identified with learning disabilities and another eight in referral process for identification as learning disabled. This was a complex mix of children with varied needs.

It was after the second graders heard Carol's voice in a segment she did for the Critical Literacy in Practice Podcast (www.clippodcast.com), which I host, that the children first started asking questions about podcasting. Carol shared their curiosity with me after which time I sent her links of children who were podcasting, such as Halloween Boy (quirkynomads .com/wp/2007/08/02/halloween-boy/) and the Children of Selsted School (www.bazmakaz.com/clip/2006/10/16/save-our-school-_-clip-15/). The Halloween Boy podcast is made by an 8-year-old boy who shares topics that are interesting to him. In his show he shares stories he retells or that he has made up himself along with tips such as how to make bubbles. The Children of Selsted is the story of a small school in England that was earmarked for closure where the students and parent community wrote, performed, and sold copies online of a song, "Save Our School" to keep their school open. Their song was picked up and played by podcasters across the globe, resulting in raising enough funds to keep the school open. Hearing other children's voices through the Internet generated more interest and conversation. It was one of these conversations that led to the children's desire to start a podcast of their own.

100% Kids: Podcasting and Identity Work

After much deliberation, the children decided they wanted to share on the podcast those issues they had been taking up that focus on fairness and injustice, not to take the moral high ground but to make accessible to potential listeners—both kids and adults—how they have attempted to contribute to change in different spaces and places. Following further conversation, they decided to call their show 100% Kids to indicate that they (the children) would generate the topics to be discussed on the show and that the voices you would hear on the show would primarily be theirs. Some of the topics they addressed in their show include animal rights, global/environmental issues, being positioned as powerless (as in the decision to cancel a school trip that the second graders had been excited to attend), and dealing with identity work (such as the ways in which some of the children who were hesitant to participate in class activities were able to take on more prominent roles in the classroom as a result of taking on the role of podcaster).

Having decided on a focus for the show, the next step was to contact the children's parents/guardians to let them know about the project and to have them sign permission forms. With the consent of all the parents, the podcast project was quickly on its way. We also talked with the children about radio names or show names. Carol had a discussion with them about issues related to safety as the primary reason for taking on different roles and identities online. This helped the children to understand that anyone can assume a different identity online, which is why we always need to be careful of whom to trust and to be mindful of when we need to be cautious. The children were, therefore, not naïve to the existence of other people online that may not have their best interests in mind. Carol spoke with them about not blindly trusting people they met online, including those who may comment on their podcast. We did, however, take extra precautions and monitored the comments so that any inappropriate ones were deleted. In the case of 100% Kids, other than some spam e-mail, all of the comments were appropriate. (For information on online safety, go to www .microsoft.com/protect/family/guidelines/predators.mspx)

The act of choosing radio names was very exciting as children were quick to realize that taking on these new names meant the ability to also construct new identities. Gee (2004, 2005) talks about new technology, like podcasting, as opening up possibilities for new forms of interacting that are quite motivating and compelling. For some, the act of renaming themselves into an alternate existence was transformative, and once shy and hesitant children for whom the curriculum was difficult to access were taking on new roles in the classroom. This fits Nixon and Gutiérrez's (2008) notion of identity play whereby children are able to extend the ways in which they are able to express themselves and tell their stories. As they play with language for publication in the online space, they develop an authorial stance or point of view from which they communicate their ideas. In doing so, they develop new identities as meaning makers (Nixon & Gutiérrez, 2008).

Maria, a shy, withdrawn 7-year-old identified with multiple learning issues was one such child. When I first met her, she deliberately shied away from me and in fact she was rarely ever in the classroom when I was there. She barely spoke and did not have much to do with the other children, including their podcasting. In her journal, Carol wrote,

> Maria developed many difficulties with learning, speech, and hearing. Queen came to my class with an IEP [Individual Education Plan] for social skills and speech and language which barely touched on how much more there was to learn about her struggles with learning. She mostly liked to be alone and work alone which stood out to me. I also could not understand what she said and this dilemma was true for many of the students in the class as well. There were many abrupt "what?!" from her classmates when we introduced ourselves in the first days [of school]. She tried hard, but much of what came out of her was not understandable. The kids wanted to know about her favorite foods and colors, so their questioning was in her best interests, but still hurt Maria because she was trying so hard to make herself understood.
>
> While Maria's classmates could not understand her, she could not always understand them either. Maria has partial hearing loss and uses an amplifying unit so that she can better hear and understand what someone is saying in whole-group sessions. I wore a microphone on days when I knew I could not speak as loud as I could. Mary had a seat on the rug next to me if we were in a circle or if we were in a group lesson, she had a place in the front. Still, I watched Maria just escape into her own world as lessons went too fast or if she was tired from the night before or from the amount of focus she needed to keep in order to comprehend what was going on. Maria had plenty of struggles to manage throughout the year.

I spent one to two mornings a week in the classroom during the fall 2006 and spring 2007. Maria would sit or stand along the periphery of the classroom. Slowly, she began watching what her classmates were doing and she started to listen in on some of their conversation. Eventually she listened, with the other children, to one of their shows. After having heard a couple of shows she became more and more interested and gave herself a radio name. She wanted to be known as Queen, a nickname her mom called her. This was a name that apparently made her feel good, safe, and wanted.

Prior to our first recording session, I talked with Queen about the equipment I was using and reassured her that we could record as many times as she wanted. My first recording session with Queen lasted about 15 minutes. Queen's debut performance consisted of one line, "We hope you like our painting of the world," which would be part of the art section of the podcast where there was a brief discussion regarding the piece of art used in the show notes.

It took six or seven takes and approximately 25 minutes of editing to produce what amounted to Queen's 2.5 seconds of audio. If this were another task she would have given up on it or not participated at all, but Queen hung in there. I had explained to her that we could cut out the pieces she wasn't happy with and leave in the pieces she likes. Knowing these editing tools were available, according to Gee (2003), lowered the consequences of failure and created a space for Maria to take on this new challenge.

Several shows later a different Queen emerged as she physically and emotionally moved from the periphery of the classroom to the center where classmates were. No longer was she recording with me as an individual child, she was now recording and engaging in banter with a group of girls. In subsequent episodes, Maria can be heard singing songs which she helped create with her classmates and saying things like "You go, girl" or "That's right, girl." In her identity as Queen she was able to position herself as part of a group of classmates who by the end of the year had become her friends. No program of study or mandated curriculum could have helped her with this. For Queen, the experience of podcasting was as transformative for her as it was for other children in the class.

Part of organizing the show included deciding on what segments to include. The children wanted an introduction to prepare their audience for listening to the show. They also wanted to have an art piece to post on the podcast homepage. The art piece was to represent the salient issues from the show. When possible, they wanted to include a song or two in connection with the topics to be discussed. They also decided on including a news segment or current events segment, a dedication piece, and finally an acknowledgment section.

Putting Together a Show

Recognizing the cross-curricular work that was part of putting together a show helped Carol to not limit the amount of time spent on crafting the scripts. Some days she and her students worked for 30 minutes and other days they spent the whole morning researching, writing, and revising. This was possible because Carol recognized the ways in which the work they were doing with podcasting cut across different content areas (see Table 15 for examples). She was, therefore, not worried about not having time to cover other areas of the second-grade curriculum. Throughout the process, they used the library and online resources to research their topics or themes.

From Monday to Thursday the children generated ideas for the show, choosing themes or topics to address based on their interests and inquiry questions. Some of these ideas were generated through their conversations and experiences outside of school, while other ideas were generated as they worked with various multimedia texts including children's books. The children would write, revise, perform, and then revise again their various scripts until they had crafted a text they felt was meaningful to share with an audience. To do this they often asked for one another's opinions. They worked collaboratively in small groups drawing on one another's knowledge of particular topics or events and researching particular bits of information. They shared ideas with one another and helped one another in many ways. The parents/guardians played a role by helping with translating some of the episodes to Spanish.

Based on their interests and desires, as the children moved to doing different parts of the show, they mentored and ushered one another along. In a way they were doing what Gee (2003) refers to as a debugging of their experiences, thereby learning from the experiences of others as they took on new roles or exchanged roles in the production of the show. Knowledge

Table 15. Examples of How the Podcast Work Cut Across Different Content Areas

Content Area	Standards of Learning	Literacies Produced Through Podcasting Work
Oral language, reading, and writing	2.3. The student will use oral communication skills. 2.9. The student will demonstrate comprehension of information in reference materials. 2.11. The student will write stories, letters, and simple explanations.	Producing a show involved • Researching topics • Writing scripts: narrative, reports, jokes, songs, introductions, dedications, acknowledgments • Rehearsing scripts • Performing on the show and taking on different identities • Critiquing and evaluating their performances • Reading and responding to comments
Science	2.4. The student will investigate and understand that plants and animals undergo a series of orderly changes in their life cycles. 2.5. The student will investigate and understand that living things are part of a system.	Science-based topics explored include • Global warming • Endangered species • Sea and ocean life • Other environmental issues
Math	2.18 The student will use calendar language appropriately (e.g., months, *today, yesterday, next week, last week*); determine past and future days of the week; and identify specific dates on a given calendar.	Producing a show involved • Creating timelines and schedules • Meeting deadlines • Prioritizing and ordering elements of the show • Deciding on possible topics to discuss on particular dates • Timing show episodes and scripts
Social studies	2.10c. The student will explain the responsibilities of a good citizen, with emphasis on describing actions that can improve the school and community.	The focus of the show was creating space to contribute to positive change in the community and beyond.

(continued)

Table 15. Examples of How the Podcast Work Cut Across Different Content Areas (Continued)

Content Area	Standards of Learning	Literacies Produced Through Podcasting Work
Technology research tools	C/T K-2.5. The student will use technology to locate, evaluate, and collect information from a variety of sources.	The children used technology as a tool for research, representing, and presenting information.

Standards based on the Virginia Standards of Learning: Virginia Department of Education. (n.d.). *Standards of learning currently in effect for Virginia public schools*. Retrieved July 8, 2009, from www.doe.virginia.gov/VDOE/Superintendent/Sols/home.shtml

was shared and distributed among the children, and groups were often cross functional. What this meant was that children did not always stick to working with the same group of classmates; they had no problems with creating and re-creating new groups depending on which part of the show they were interested in developing. Children like Maria, who at the start of the year had difficulty accessing learning, were able to take on different identities in the podcasting world that created space for them to participate in ways they hadn't previously.

Putting together a show wasn't always easy. To attempt to put out a weekly show is quite an undertaking but the children took on this challenge with excitement and without hesitation. This included researching their topics using both fiction and nonfiction books and electronic resources. This is consistent with two of Gee's (2003) principles of learning: Committed Learning Principle and Practice Principle. The first deals with learners participating in extended engagements, while the second deals with the ongoing rehearsing and rewriting of scripts where the repetitive nature of taking on each step of producing the show, week after week, never seemed to become boring for the child.

On Fridays, we would record the show one segment at a time. The children were quick to learn that using a digital recorder meant we could do as many takes as needed and that we could edit out extraneous artifacts and misreadings. Ben stated, "I would be surprised if in this day and age with what we can do with technology if we couldn't do that kind of editing." After recording the show, I edited the pieces together over the weekend and then released the show on the following Monday (see Figure 20 for Show Notes). To listen to the show go to www.bazmakaz.com/100kids. Mondays were not only spent listening to the show as a group but also was a time to critique the audio (see Figure 21 for a student's critique of the show) and make adjustments to the upcoming episodes. In Figure 21, the column on the left represents the segments of the show that the children think should be continued or elements that should be added. The column on the right represents things the children feel they need to work on in order to produce a quality show.

It was during their critique of the show that the children came up with the idea of incorporating a jokes segment to give their audience a break from having to listen to the important issues and topics discussed in other segments of the show. They introduced this segment in Show #2.

Liam: Hi my name is Drake. We are here to introduce a new part of the show called Jokey, Joke, Jokes.

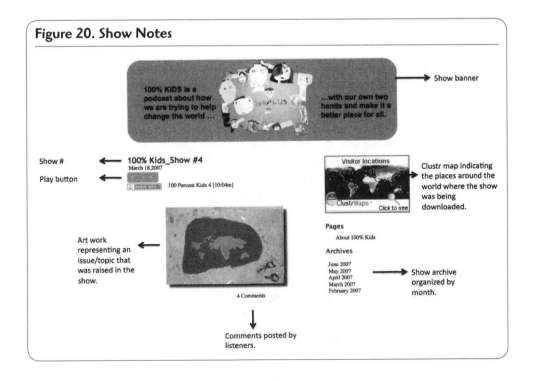

Figure 20. Show Notes

Figure 21. Critique of the Show

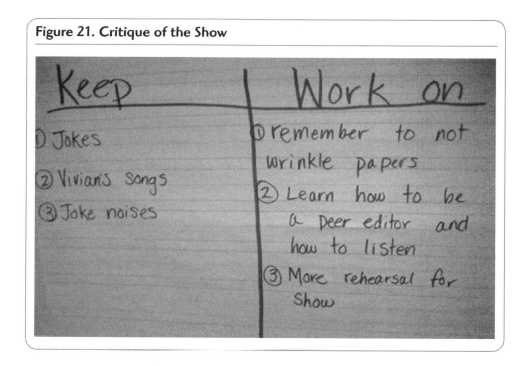

Keep

① Jokes

② Vivian's Songs

③ Joke noises

Work on

① remember to not wrinkle papers

② Learn how to be a peer editor and how to listen

③ More rehearsal for Show

Edwin C:	We think this is important to make you laugh and give you a break from listening to all this hard work.
Edwin G:	The jokes give us a break from all the hard work too!
Liam:	Here we go! I hope your stomach doesn't hurt too much from laughing!

We Did It and So Can You!

The title of this section refers to Show #8 where the children reported on a yearlong project the children took on to enable the second graders in the school to go on a trip to the Baltimore Aquarium, after the school administration had decided the trip was too costly. Coming to second grade, the children had anticipated this year-end trip. The trip was especially important for some of the kids who, because of financial constraints in their homes, were counting on this trip as their only opportunity to go to the aquarium. Being told this tradition was no longer to be continued was very problematic, and it resulted in Carol's students taking social action to reverse this decision by organizing a series of fund-raising events. Their work involved using the Internet to research what they could learn from going to the aquarium, figuring out costs for the trip including entrance fees and transportation and so forth. They also met with the principal on two occasions to discuss their displeasure at having the trip cancelled and to lay out a plan of action. They engaged in multiple activities to make the trip happen. They talked about their work, sharing sentiments of amazement and joy, in their show.

> Kia: Hi, I'm Kia. We went to the Baltimore Aquarium. That's what we did on May 8, Tuesday. Our class finally got the whole second grade to go to the Baltimore Aquarium. I think it's amazing how a bunch of second graders got all the second graders in our school to go to the Baltimore Aquarium. It's all so wonderful. Bye.

Figure 22 is the post for Show #8. It includes letters written to Carol's class thanking them for all their hard work in succeeding to send the second graders on a trip to the Baltimore Aquarium. Also included were comments from listeners congratulating the children on their accomplishment.

Connecting Across Time and Place

I was with the children as they listened to their final show of the year. The celebration included both family and friends. One of the mothers approached me, asking,

> Parent: Are you Vivian?
> Me: Yes, I am.
> Parent: I have to say thank you for doing this [podcasting] with the kids.

With tears in her eyes she continued, "My family doesn't live together because we cannot. Her father, he lives in Columbia. He waits for this [podcast] each week so he can hear her [his daughter's voice]."

Apparently, the release of each episode was the highlight of the week for him. He listened to the show at an Internet café in Columbia along

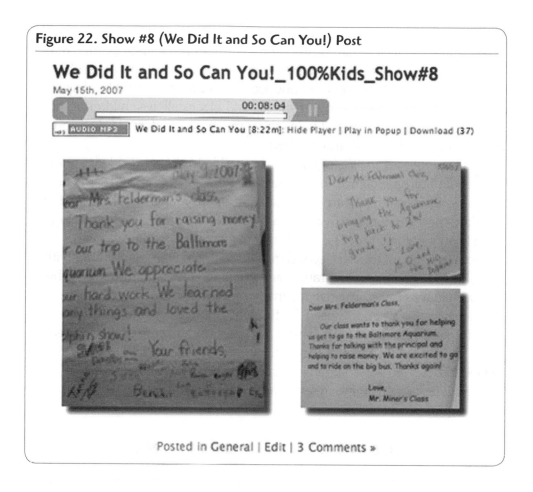

Figure 22. Show #8 (We Did It and So Can You!) Post

We Did It and So Can You!_100%Kids_Show#8

May 15th, 2007

00:08:04

AUDIO MP3 | We Did It and So Can You [8:22m]: Hide Player | Play in Popup | Download (37)

Posted in General | Edit | 3 Comments »

with other family members. The family had been divided and living in different countries as a way to create a better life for themselves. It was an extraordinary surprise to discover that the children's podcast had this kind of impact.

For the children, producing, designing, and redesigning episodes and segments included in their podcast created a space to get at the notion that texts are socially constructed and that literacy is most definitely not a neutral technology. Through the issues they researched and talked about on the show, as well as through their own experiences in learning about how they each could contribute to this shared experience, they learned about ways they are positioned within certain social systems and the discursive practices or ways of being, doing, speaking, and acting that shape these and the ways in which they position others through the choices they make. They learned to use what the technology afforded them to reach and connect with people beyond the physical limitations of their school site. Connecting with people in other spaces and places allows children to hear the perspective of others and helps them make more informed decisions as participants of the world around them.

The use of new technology made accessible to them knowledge that they could not have gained in a pretechnological age. For instance, while using the Internet, they learned about what other young people have done in other spaces and places using social networking tools like podcasting.

Throughout this process, students drew from their cultural and semiotic resources, moved beyond more traditional ways of working with texts, including children's literature and creating texts, and in the end the experience was transformative for many of them. Podcasting and new technologies became tools used for thinking about the world and for learning and communicating as well as representing some critical literacy work that takes into account the stuff of everyday life, everyday social issues and events, and children's existing literacy practices, and that creates opportunities for engaging in social action projects.

REFLECTION QUESTIONS

1. In what ways do you currently use technology in your setting? In what ways do your students currently use technology in their everyday lives? What kinds of resources, support, hardware, and software do you imagine you would need to explore the use of technology in your setting?

2. What might get in the way of your using technology? How might you get past this hurdle?

3. What sorts of technological tools are you interested in using? To do what kind of work and for what purpose?

4. In what ways are you interested in connecting with others via the Internet? For what reasons? For what purpose(s)?

5. What might you do differently with the use of technology? What might your students be able to do differently?

New Directions and Curricular Possibilities for Doing "Important Work"

Teacher:	I can't believe that it's already June.
Patricia:	Yeah. September, October, November...June.
Alexandro:	Lots of months, lots of learning.
Emma:	And lots of books. I like books.
Alexandro:	Yes...books and more books.
Teacher:	What are some things you've learned about books this year?
Alexandro:	When we talked about books, mostly we talked about us.
Teacher:	Tell me more about that.
Emma:	Not just words, right?
Patricia:	Right. Mostly our talk and using words and pictures to do important work like changing what's not fair.
Alexandro:	Sometimes that's hard, but sometimes not so hard.
Patricia:	But that's important work, right, Emma?
Emma:	Right, Patricia.

It is the end of the school year. My kindergarten students whom you met at the beginning of this book sat informally chatting about the year that had passed. Their talk focused on their work with books and how that work was sometimes hard and sometimes not so hard, but most important they understood they had done important work to contribute to changing "what's not fair."

The "important work" that Patricia and Emma referred to in this exchange includes the experiences we had with all sorts of texts—using texts not just for pleasure or enjoyment but also for creating spaces to understand how language works to construct people, for using language to critique the word and the world, and for changing social practices that give an advantage to some people over others. By adopting a critical pedagogy that made it possible for my students and me to investigate the positions taken up by texts, I was able to help my students become literate beings who question things that are taken for granted or are assumed to be normal or natural in the world (see Table 16 for resources on critical literacy in practice). My students and I did this by critically reading and analyzing the world in which we live. We analyzed the things with which we agreed and disagreed, and we imagined new or revised versions of those things.

If you recall, I opened this book with a conversation between Patricia and Alexandro regarding their disappointment in discovering that there were no books about the Philippines in our school library even though there were large numbers of Filipino students in our school. Their concern was mainly for their new classmate, Emma, who had just arrived from the Philippines. Therefore, it is ironic to notice that in the previous conversation it was Emma who noted that books are "not just words, right?"

The teachers whose classrooms you visited in this book share Emma's sentiments that books and other texts are "not just words." In each of their classrooms, books were more than tools for learning language and learning about language. They used books as one of several tools for using language to critique, and in so doing, to question, interrogate, problematize, denaturalize, interrupt, and disrupt that which appears normal, natural, ordinary, mundane, and everyday, as well as to redesign, reconstruct, reimagine, rethink, and reconsider social worlds, spaces, and places. Using language to critique helped each of us to understand that books and other texts, including multimedia texts, are ideological sites or spaces for systemic values to reside. The reality of the ever-increasing number of multimedia images that we come across in a given day was one of the reasons that necessitated the creation of this second edition, which includes, among other things, a discussion on technology and what new technology affords the work we do in schools. As Gee (2004) points out, "These new technologies and media may well recruit forms of thinking, interacting, and valuing that are quite different from—and again, more compelling and

Table 16. Resources on Critical Literacy in Practice

Comber, B., & Simpson, A. (2001). *Negotiating critical literacies in classrooms.* Mahwah, NJ: Erlbaum.

Comber, B., & Thomson, P., (with Wells, M.). (2001). Critical literacy finds a "place": Writing and social action in a low income Australian grade 2/3 classroom. *The Elementary School Journal, 101*(4), 451–464.

Edelsky, C. (Ed.). (2000). *Making justice our project: Teachers working toward critical whole language practice.* Urbana, IL: National Council of Teachers of English.

Fehring, H., & Green, P. (Eds.). (2001). *Critical literacy: A collection of articles from the Australian Literacy Educators' Association.* Newark, DE: International Reading Association.

Heffernan, L., & Lewison, M. (2000). Making real-world issues our business: Critical literacy in a third-grade classroom. *Primary Voices K–6, 9*(2), 15–21.

Janks, H. (2000). Domination, access, diversity, and design: A synthesis for critical literacy education. *Educational Review, 52*(2), 175–186.

Janks, H., & Comber, B. (2005) Critical literacy across continents. In K. Pahl & J. Rowsell (Eds.), *Travel notes from the new literacy studies: Instances of practice* (pp. 95–117). Clevedon, UK: Multilingual Matters.

Larson, J., & Marsh, J. (2005). *Making literacy real: Theories and practices for learning and teaching.* Thousand Oaks, CA: Sage.

Luke, A. (2007). The new literacies. *Webcasts and podcasts for educators.* Retrieved January 20, 2009, from www.curriculum.org/secretariat/may31.shtml

Marsh, J. (2000). "But I want to fly too!": Girls and superhero play in the infant classroom. *Gender and Education, 12*(2), 209–220.

Mellor, B., O'Neill, M., & Patterson, A. (2000). *Reading stories: Activities and texts for critical readings.* Urbana, IL: National Council of Teachers of English.

Morgan, W. (1997). *Critical literacy in the classroom: The art of the possible.* New York: Routledge.

Muspratt, S., Luke, A., & Freebody, P. (1997). *Constructing critical literacies: Teaching and learning textual practice.* Cresskill, NJ: Hampton.

O'Brien, J. (1994). Show Mum you love her: Taking a new look at junk mail. *Reading, 28*(1), 43–46.

Vasquez, V. (1998). Building equitable communities: Taking social action in a kindergarten classroom. *Talking Points, 9*(2), 3–6.

Vasquez, V. (2000a). Building community through social action. *School Talk, 5*(4), 2–3.

Vasquez, V. (2000b). Language stories and critical literacy lessons. *Talking Points, 11*(2), 5–7.

Vasquez, V. (2000c). Our way: Using the everyday to create a critical literacy curriculum. *Primary Voices, 9*(2), 8–13.

Vasquez, V. (2003). What Pokemon can teach us about learning and literacy. *Language Arts, 81*(2), 118–125.

Vasquez, V. (2004). *Negotiating critical literacies with young children.* Mahwah, NJ: Erlbaum.

motivating than—those children find in today's schools" (p. 38). What this means is that these tools could help children to increase their repertoires of literacy practices, including children with diverse abilities and children who are linguistically and culturally diverse. As noted by Nixon and Gutiérrez (2008), multimedia literacy learning, such as digital storytelling,

> allows children who are at a developmental age when issues of identity are particularly salient, to reflect on questions of who they are and who they might become creating space for them to engage in identity play with events in their lives and their future possible selves. (p. 123)

Together, I and the teachers whose stories I share in this book grew to understand that the point of reading the "word" and the "world" against the grain, such as discussing various issues from different perspectives, is to help illuminate topics associated with power and control such as racism and gender inequity to create spaces to take action in and on the world and in so doing to participate differently in that world as literate beings, young and old. The addition of technology further illuminates the ways in which we might participate in the world.

We were at different places in our conceptualization of critical literacy as I created this book. Given a different time and space, different stories may have been told, and different texts may have been used to practice the use of language in more powerful ways. One common denominator in each of our stories, however, is that all of us attempted to create spaces in our particular locations to engage in the "important work" referred to by Patricia and Emma. I hope that this book helps you to do the same.

Getting Started
. . . .
Through writing different accounts of working with books in K–6 classrooms, I intended to share not only successes and pleasures, but also tensions. I hope the stops and starts were visible to you as you read through the pages of this book, and that reflecting on the work I shared provided you with a space for thinking about ways of working critically with books written for children, as well as other texts. The instances of learning presented in the previous pages were not meant as definitive answers for "doing" critical literacy using children's books. Rather, they were examples of attempts at finding spaces for critical literacies through using children's

books in combination with other texts, and technology, as one way to begin to make accessible to students a metalanguage to challenge the potential of texts to impose limited ways of thinking about the world. I hope that the different accounts of critical work with books and other texts provide you with opportunities to think differently about the role that children's literature can play in a classroom, and that you are able to find space to begin engaging in critical literacies.

REFLECTION QUESTIONS

1. Now that you have had a chance to read about possibilities for working differently with books from a critical literacy perspective, what are some possibilities that you have imagined for working from this perspective in your setting?

2. What can you imagine to be possible road blocks and how might you get beyond such barriers? What resources and support would be helpful for you?

3. How might you make accessible to others the work that you do so that they may learn from your experience?

REFERENCES

Barton, D., & Hamilton, M. (1998). *Local literacies: Reading and writing in one community.* London: Routledge.

Bigelow, W., Christensen, L., Karp, S., Miner, B., & Peterson, B. (1994). *Rethinking our classrooms: Teaching for equity and justice.* Milwaukee, WI: Rethinking Schools.

Buckingham, D., & Sefton-Green, J. (1995). *Cultural studies goes to school: Reading and teaching popular media.* London: Taylor & Francis.

Burke, C.L. (1997). *Using trade books in the classroom.* Graduate seminar, Indiana University, Bloomington, IN.

Christensen, L. (2000). *Reading, writing, and rising up: Teaching about social justice and the power of the written word.* Milwaukee, WI: Rethinking Schools.

Comber, B. (1992). Critical literacy: A selective review and discussion of the recent literature. *South Australian Educational Leader, 3*(1), 1–10.

Comber, B. (2001). Critical literacies and local action: Teacher knowledge and a new research agenda. In B. Comber & A. Simpson (Eds.), *Negotiating critical literacies in classrooms* (pp. 271–282). Mahwah, NJ: Erlbaum.

Comber, B. (2005). Interview with Barbara Comber. In J. Larson & J. Marsh (Eds.), *Making literacy real: Theories and practices for learning and teaching* (pp. 61–67). Thousand Oaks, CA: Sage.

Comber, B., Nixon, H., & Reid, J. (Eds.). (2007). *Literacies in place: Teaching environmental communications.* Newtown, NSW, Australia: Primary English Teachers Association.

Comber, B., & Simpson, A. (Eds.). (2001). *Negotiating critical literacies in classrooms.* Mahwah, NJ: Erlbaum.

Comber, B., & Thomson, P. (with Wells, M.). (2001). Critical literacy finds a "place": Writing and social action in a low-income Australian grade 2/3 classroom. *The Elementary School Journal, 101*(4), 451–464. doi:10.1086/499681

The Diffusion Group (2005, May). *Podcasting as an extension of portable digital media: Fact, fiction, and opportunity.* Retrieved September 8, 2006, from www.marketresearch.com/product/display.asp?productid=1150638&g=1

Edelsky, C. (Ed.). (2000). *Making justice our project: Teachers working toward critical whole language practice.* Urbana, IL: National Council of Teachers of English.

Egawa, K., & Harste, J.C. (2001). Balancing the literary curriculum: A new vision. *School Talk, 7*(1), 1–8.

Epstein, D. (1993). *Changing classroom cultures: Anti-racism, politics, and schools.* Stoke-on-Trent, England: Trentham.

Fiske, J. (1989). *Reading the popular.* London: Routledge.

Flint, A.S., & Riordan-Karlsson, M. (2001). *Buried treasures in the classroom: Using hidden influences to enhance literacy teaching and learning.* Newark, DE: International Reading Association.

Frank, B. (2008, July). *Critical literacies.* Keynote presented at the International Literacy Educators Research Network Summer Workshop, Toronto, Canada.

Freire, P. (1972). *Pedagogy of the oppressed* (M.B. Ramos, Trans.). London: Sheed and Ward.

Freire, P., & Macedo, D. (1987). *Literacy: Reading the word and the world*. South Hadley, MA: Bergin & Garvey.

Galda, L., Rayburn, S., & Stanzi, L.C. (2000). *Looking through the faraway end: Creating a literature-based reading curriculum with second graders*. Newark, DE: International Reading Association.

Gavin, J. (2009). Global Internet audience surpasses 1 billion visitors. Retrieved January 3, 2009, from. www.comscore.com/Press_Events/Press_Releases/2009/1/Global_Internet_Audience_1_Billion

Gee, J.P. (2003). *What video games have to teach us about learning and literacy*. New York, NY: Palgrave Macmillan.

Gee, J.P. (2004). *Situated language and learning: A critique of traditional schooling*. London: Routledge.

Gee, J.P. (2005). *An introduction to discourse analysis: Theory and method* (2nd ed.). New York: Routledge.

Granville, S. (1993). *Language, advertising, and power*. Johannesburg, South Africa: Witwatersrand University Press.

Haas Dyson, A. (2005). Foreword. In J. Evans, *Literacy moves on: Popular culture, new technologies, and critical literacy in the elementary classroom* (pp. ix–xi). Portsmouth, NH: Heinemann..

Harste, J.C. (1997, July). *Curriculum as audit trail: Underlying premises*. Paper presented at the Whole Language Umbrella Conference, Rochester, New York.

Harste, J.C. (2001, July). The Halliday Plus Model. Presentation given at the 2001 InterLERN workshop, Mississauga, Ontario, Canada.

Harste, J.C. (2003). What do we mean by literacy now? *Voices From the Middle, 10*(3), pp. 8–12.

Harste, J.C., Leland, C., Lewison, M., Ociepka, A., & Vasquez, V. (2000). Supporting critical conversations in classrooms. In K.M. Pierce (Ed.), *Adventuring with books: A booklist for pre-K–grade 6* (pp. 507–512). Urbana, IL: National Council of Teachers of English.

Heffernan, L., & Lewison, M. (2000). Making real-world issues our business: Critical literacy in a third-grade classroom. *Primary Voices K–6, 9*(2), 15–21.

Heger, D. (2000). *The other meaning of Arbor Day*. Retrieved on January 8, 2009, from www.mackinac.org/article.aspx?ID=4126

Janks, H. (1993). *Language, identity, & power*. Johannesburg, South Africa: Witwatersrand University Press.

Janks, H. (2000). Domination, access, diversity, and design: A synthesis for critical literacy education. *Educational Review, 52*(2), 175–186. doi:10.1080/713664035

Janks, H., & Comber, B. (2005). Critical literacy across continents. In K. Pahl & J. Rowsell (Eds.), *Travel notes from the new literacy studies: Instances of practice* (pp. 95–117). Clevedon, UK: Multilingual Matters.

Johnston, P. (2004). *Choice words: How our language affects children's learning*. Portland, ME: Stenhouse.

Lankshear, C., & Knobel, M. (2007). *A new literacies sampler*. New York: Peter Lang.

Larson, J., & Marsh, J. (2005). *Making literacy real: Theories and practices for learning and teaching*. Thousand Oaks, CA: Sage.

Lasseter, J., & Ranft, J. (Directors). (2006). *Cars* [Motion picture]. United States: Disney Pixar Productions.

Lee, H. (2006). *Podcast statistics: Researches, studies and other interesting data.* The Marketing Loop. Retrieved April 20, 2006, from podcastingscout.com/podcast -statistics

Luke, A. (2007). The new literacies. *Webcasts and podcasts for educators.* Toronto, ON: Curriculum Services Canada. Retrieved January 20, 2009, from www.curriculum.org/ secretariat/may31.shtml

Luke, A., & Freebody, P. (1997). Shaping the social practices of reading. In S. Muspratt, A. Luke, & P. Freebody (Eds.), *Constructing critical literacies: Teaching and learning textual practice* (pp. 185–226). Cresskill, NJ: Hampton.

Luke, A., & Freebody, P. (1999). Further notes on the four resources model. *Reading Online.* Retrieved July 15, 2000, from www.readingonline.org/research/lukefreebody .html

Manning, A. (1993). Curriculum as conversation. In A. Manning, *Foundations of literacy* (pp. 48–60). Halifax, Nova Scotia: Mount Saint Vincent University.

Marsh, J. (Ed.). (2005). *Popular culture, new media and digital literacy in early childhood.* New York: Routledge Falmer.

Meacham, S.J. (2003, March). *Literacy and street credibility: Plantations, prisons, and African American literacy from Frederick Douglass to Fifty Cent.* Presentation at the Economic and Social Research Council Seminar Series Conference, Sheffield, United Kingdom.

Moll, L.C. (1992). Funds of knowledge for teaching: Using a qualitative approach to connect homes and classrooms. *Theory Into Practice, 31*(1), 132–141.

Morgan, W. (1997). *Critical literacy in the classroom: The art of the possible.* New York: Routledge.

Nixon, A.S., & Gutiérrez, K. (2008). Digital literacies for young English learners: Productive pathways toward equity and robust learning. In C. Genishi & A.L. Goodwin (Eds.), *Diversities in early childhood education: rethinking and doing* (pp. 121–136). New York: Routledge.

O'Brien, J. (2001). Children reading critically: A local history. In B. Comber & A. Simpson (Eds.), *Negotiating critical literacies in classrooms* (pp. 37–54). Mahwah, NJ: Erlbaum.

Oxford University Press. (2005). *"Podcast" is the word of the year.* Retrieved November 15, 2007, from www.us.oup.com/us/brochure/NOAD_podcast/

Poole, S.M. (2004). History colors Aboriginal artist's life: Mural in East Atlanta reflects Australia's racist past. Retrieved July 7, 2009, from www.eniar.org/news/ajc.html

Schmidt, K. (1998, August). *Math investigations.* Presentation given at the 1998 InterLERN workshop, Mississauga, Ontario, Canada.

Shor, I., & Freire, P. (1987). *A pedagogy for liberation: Dialogues on transforming education.* South Hadley, MA: Bergin & Garvey.

Short, K.G., Harste, J.C., & Burke, C.L. (1996). *Creating classrooms for authors and inquirers.* Portsmouth, NH: Heinemann.

Vasquez, V. (1994). A step in the dance of critical literacy. *UKRA Reading, 28*(1), 39–43. doi:10.1111/j.1467-9345.1994.tb00115.x

Vasquez, V. (1998). Building equitable communities: Taking social action in a kindergarten classroom. *Talking Points, 9*(2), 3–6.

Vasquez, V. (1999). *Negotiating critical literacies with young children.* Unpublished doctoral dissertation, Indiana University, Bloomington.

Vasquez, V. (2000a). Building community through social action. *School Talk, 5*(4), 2–3.

Vasquez, V. (2000b). Language stories and critical literacy lessons. *Talking Points, 11*(2), 5–7.

Vasquez, V. (2000c). Our way: Using the everyday to create a critical literacy curriculum. *Primary Voices, 9*(2), 8–13.

Vasquez, V. (2001a). *Creating a critical literacy curriculum with young children* (Phi Delta Kappa International Research Bulletin No. 29). Bloomington, IN: Phi Delta Kappa.

Vasquez, V. (2001b). Negotiating critical literacies in elementary classrooms. In B. Comber & A. Simpson (Eds.), *Critical literacy at elementary sites* (pp. 55–58). Mahwah, NJ: Erlbaum.

Vasquez, V. (2003a). *Using the everyday: Constructing critical literacies with young children*. Mahwah, NJ: Erlbaum.

Vasquez, V. (2003b). What Pokemon can teach us about learning and literacy. *Language Arts, 81*(2), 118–125.

Vasquez, V. (2004). *Negotiating critical literacies with young children*. Mahwah, NJ: Erlbaum.

Vasquez, V. (2005). Resistance, power-tricky, and colorless energy: What engagement with everyday popular culture texts can teach us about learning, and literacy. In J. Marsh (Ed.), *Popular culture, new media and digital literacy in early childhood* (pp. 201–218). New York: Routledge Falmer.

Vasquez, V., Egawa, K., Harste, J.C., & Thompson, R. (Eds.). (2004). *Literacy as social practice: Primary voices K-6*. Urbana, IL: National Council of Teachers of English.

Virginia Department of Education. (n.d.). *Standards of learning currently in effect for Virginia public schools*. Retrieved November 1, 2008, from www.doe.virginia.gov/VDOE/Superintendent/Sols/home.shtml

Watson, D., Burke, C.L., & Harste, J.C. (1989). *Whole language: Inquiring voices*. New York: Scholastic.

Whitin, D.J., & Whitin, P. (2004). *New visions for linking literature and mathematics*. Urbana, IL: National Council of Teachers of English; Reston, VA: National Council of Teachers of Mathematics.

Whitin, D.J., & Whitin, P. (2005). *What if we changed the book? Problem-posing with sixteen cows*. Retrieved June 16, 2009, from www.readwritethink.org/lessons/lesson_view.asp?id=815

Whitin, P., & Whitin, D.J. (2000). *Math is language too: Talking and writing in the mathematics classroom*. Urbana, IL: National Council of Teachers of English; Reston, VA: National Council of Teachers of Mathematics.

Zeccola, J. (2001). *Human rights and equal opportunity commission report*. Australian Bureau of Statistics 2001 Census.

CHILDREN'S LITERATURE CITED

Baguley, E. (2005). *Meggie Moon*. Intercourse, PA: Good Books.

Best, C. (2006). *Sally Jean, the bicycle queen*. New York: Farrar Straus Giroux.

Browne, A. (1990). *Piggybook*. New York: Knopf.

Childerhose, R.J. (1981). The hockey story. In C. Graves & C. McClymont (Eds.). *Contexts: Anthology one*. Scarborough, Ontario: Nelson Canada.

Clement, R. (1991). *Counting on Frank*. Milwaukee, WI: Gareth Stevens.

Cole, B. (1997). *Princess Smartypants*. New York: Putnam.

Dipuchio, K. (2008). *Grace for President*. New York: Disney Book Group/Hyperion.

Fleischman, P. (2004). *Seed folks*. New York: Harper Teen.

Love, D.A. (2006). *Of numbers and stars: The story of Hypatia*. New York: Holiday House.

Lovell, P., & Catrow, D. (2002). *Stand tall, Molly Lou Melon*. New York, NY: Putnam.

Lyon, G. (1994). *Mama is a miner*. New York: Scholastic.

Mannis, C.D. (2006). *Julia Morgan built a castle*. New York: Viking.

Morrison, T., & Morrison, S. (1999). *The big box*. Burbank, CA: Disney.

Munsch, R. (1988). *The paper bag princess*. Toronto: Annick.

Peet, B. (1991). *The wump world*. New York: Houghton Mifflin.

Perry, S. (1995). *If....* Oxford, UK: Oxford University Press Children's Books.

Shange, N. (1997). *White wash*. New York: Walker.

Smith, D. (2002). *If the world were a village: A book about the world's people*. Tonawanda, NY: Kids Can Press.

Smith Milway, K. (2008). *One hen: How one small loan made a big difference*. Tonawanda, NY: Kids Can Press.

Tetro, M. (1994). *The Royal Canadian Mounted Police*. St. Laurent, Quebec: Marc Tetro Canada.

INDEX

Note. Page numbers followed by *f* or *t* indicate figures or tables, respectively.

C

CASE STUDIES, 33–34

CATROW, D., 96

CENSORSHIP, 61

CHILCOAT, G.W., 40*t*

CHILDERHOSE, R.J., 32, 34

CHILDREN: Aboriginal, 48–50, 51*f*; kindergarten students, 125; second graders, 113–124

CHILDREN HELPING CHILDREN (WEBSITE), 58*t*

CHILDREN OF SELSTED SCHOOL (WEBSITE), 113

CHILDREN'S BOOKS, 9; that can be used to discuss gender issues, 30*t*; that can be used to discuss issues of social justice and equity, 44–45; multimedia text sets in which characters and people take action, 57, 58*t*; pairing everyday texts with, 10, 23–38; pairing media texts with, 32–34; picture books, 55–57, 56*t*, 57, 58*t*; school library books, 1–2, 5–7; six-sessions strategy for working with picture books, 55–57, 56*t*

CHILDREN'S LITERATURE, 67–80; to create spaces for critically reading classroom practice, 77–79; critical use of, 10; in elementary school settings, 11; to unpack social issues, 10, 39–53

CHIOLA-NAKAI, D., 32

CHOICES, 68; suggestions for choosing books, 78

CHRISTENSEN, L., 33, 71

CLASS LETTERS, 75

CLASSROOM: critically reading classroom practices, 77–79; curricula that play out in, 23–24; inclusion classrooms, 95; setting context for social issues in, 95–96; using books in, 1–22

CLEMENT, R., 29, 30*t*, 70–77

CLOZING THE DEAL ON ARBOR DAY (ACTIVITY), 98

CODE-BREAKING PRACTICES, 14

COHN, D., 58*t*

COLE, B., 29, 30*t*

COLEMAN, E., 40*t*

COMBER, B., 2, 8, 12, 25*t*, 36, 83, 103, 109, 127*t*

COMMITTEE LEARNING PRINCIPLE, 119

COMMUNICATION: blogs, 111–112; podcast signs, 108, 108*f*; podcasts, 105–124; technology as tool for sharing work, 10; via podcasts, 122–124

COMMUNITY ISSUES: issues to take up, 47–48; using children's literature to unpack, 39–53

COMSCORE INC., 111

CONSERVATION: conversations about, 93; planting trees, 96–98

CONTROL: books for creating space to talk about, 40*t*; conversations about, 39–40; issues of, 39–53; multimedia text sets on, 48–50. *See also* Power

CONVERSATIONS: about Arbor Day, 97–101; about censorship, 61; about conservation, 93; about end-of-the-year celebrations, 67–80; about gender equity, 23–26, 47; about labels, 47; about Nike, 33; podcasts, 105–124; about power, 39–40, 42, 46–47; about power and control, 39–40; about racism, 54; about school, 125; about science curriculum, 86–89; about shame, 62–63; small-group, 56*t*, 59–62; sustained, 97–100; about uniforms, 32; about violence in books and movies, 61–62; about weather, 88–89

COUNTING ON FRANK (CLEMENT), 70–77

COURAGE, 52*t*

COWAN, K., 42*t*

L

M

R

S